FROM *Soul* TO *Soulmate:*

BRIDGES FROM NEAR-DEATH
EXPERIENCE WISDOM

BY JODY LONG

This book is dedicated to soulmates all over the world, whether they are single or in a committed relationship!

TABLE OF CONTENTS

PREFACE

This book has been a lot of fun to write. I have also had a lot of validation along the way.

For instance, I had given the chapter on soulmates to one of my dear soul sisters. She read it and fell asleep. She dreamed of her soulmate. She told me that never happens to her. Since that time, she has had three more dreams of this man . . . Time will tell. . .

I also had contacted a couple NDErs about the book. It turns out that both of them had recently met their twin-flames. Everywhere I turn, there are coincidences that make it time to share this book with you.

I have heard of many people, especially in the 50 and older category who are now meeting their soulmates. I can't help but wonder if there is a wave of love energy surrounding the planet to help balance all of the chaos, frustration, and negativity we are now experiencing on earth.

In many ways the chaos tells us that we need to remember what is truly important. We turn our attention away from the material world and look to spirit. In our relationships, we find the love and comfort to help us deal with the day to day stresses of our earthly life.

Love and our relationships with each other are the ultimate lessons. There is no time like the present to get started.

May your journey be rewarding and totally fulfilling. I wish you the very best in finding your soulmate and many blessings to you all!

Jody Long

ACKNOWLEDGEMENTS

I want to thank the many people who have helped to make this book possible. I want to thank Jeffrey Long whose efforts made the research and websites possible. I would like to extend a hearty thanks to Bill Guggenheim, for his expertise in editing, great insight, and endorsement. I also want to thank Ken Ring and Joyce Hawkes for taking the time to write on my behalf.

And I would like to thank my soul-sisters who encouraged me in this process: Alexa Hartung, Deana Chase-Moore, and Paula Pakkala. I also want to thank my family for lending their ear, encouragement and support: Carol Woodley, Kathy Rozonsky, Kory Rozonsky, and Jeri Colwill.

INTRODUCTION

Many of you may remember the commercial with the baby and the exasperated mother wishing that the stork had brought instructions. I'm sure many readers would also appreciate if potential partners came with instructions, too. Unfortunately, that isn't the case. The subject of relationships in our schools is reduced to sex education rather than concentrating on how to have a lasting, fulfilling relationship. In our homes, relationship education is what our parents tried to teach us, when most of the time they had as little clue as we did. The American myth of the ideal partner, the house with the white picket fence, and 2.4 children is reinforced with Cinderella stories and Harlequin romances. The media bombards us with violence, dysfunctional or unrealistic advice that borders on disaster, pure fantasy, or strictly-for-entertainment relationships.

I get hundreds of e-mails per year from people all over the world asking about soulmates. Many times, they are looking for validation of a soul experience or a reason to leave their spouse; sometimes they want to find their "soulmate." What I hear from people is that there needs to be more love. Most come to this realization primarily from their failed relationships. I think there is a tremendous need for an understanding of soulmates, how they work, the role of love in our lives, and ultimately, unconditional love in the world.

Whether it is a world economic downturn, youngsters starting on their own after graduation, or limited resources, the new generation will find that it is essential to live with others. There are very few lucky ones who can afford to live on their own. Most high school or college graduates cannot survive economically unless they partner and share their resources with another person. Therefore, learning about people and understanding how soulmates work is crucial to individual future happiness. Making smart choices is one key element of becoming a soulmate.

I've been a family law attorney for over twelve years. I've watched what people go through during a nasty divorce, and I've also had the opportunity to study relationships to see what goes right—even how relationships last after death. I've been actively involved in consciousness research for over a decade. I have done several studies on the website on different aspects of the near-death experience. The largest study was a five part series on soulmates. From all of this, I have come to the conclusion that all we need is love.

But how do we find love and then how do we recognize love? We are all individuals, and most of the time, we truly don't know what love is because we see it through the filter of our humanness. The love of God, Spirit, "the All," or whatever you want to call it is the purity from where we all come. But in our humanness, we have to live on earth in our earthly bodies. So how do we reconcile being of spirit and being human?

Probably the best place to start is to look at what it means to be human, and then look at what it means to be made in the image of God. From now on, I will use the word "God," but please feel free to substitute whatever word makes you feel most comfortable. It refers to the same person/concept.

A good deal of the philosophy in this book comes from studying the near-death experience (NDE). These are people who have died. When NDErs are revived, they have amazing wisdom to share with us. It is not surprising that in order to understand love and to understand soulmates, you go to the source of "soul." NDErs have been to heaven or experienced a different state of consciousness. They have direct knowledge of what the other side is like or at least a part of what the other side is like. Theirs is a world view that espouses love and is a world view without fear—*pure love*.

It is also helpful to understand the development of human consciousness. Understanding soulmates, how to bring a soulmate into your life, or how to change your relationship to a soulmate relationship can only fully be explored with a base knowledge of consciousness. Consciousness has two parts, the body and the soul. We have to understand the body in order to distinguish between what is the soul in "soul" mate.

CONSCIOUSNESS AND FEELINGS

Evolving in consciousness is about being more than a set of preprogrammed behaviors. Robert Ornstein, in *Evolution of Consciousness: The Origins of the Way We Think*, discusses how we evolved as a species and how the brain is hardwired. As *Homo sapiens*, we survived by being hardwired to notice changes. Focusing the brain on change alerts the body to potential survival threats and whether to engage the "fight or flight" reflex. The "fight or flight" reflex is at the root of the base animal emotions of fear and anger. Yet we know that the spiritual part of us is based in love. This cosmic duality sets the stage for spiritual growth.

The way the brain is hardwired is that we have hundreds of data inputs from our environment at any given moment. The brain has a screening threshold that allows only important or life-threatening thoughts to be part of our waking reality. The rest of the information is processed in the subconscious mind, below the threshold of waking reality.

The brain can be compared to a computer. We reconstruct memories and can change behaviors by accessing them through a data chunk in a file that is stored in an emotional directory. Once accessed, the brain remembers by retrieving the data chunks and stringing them together in an order that makes sense. Normally, the person's brain will fill in the gaps between data chunks, and a story is recollected. The data chunks don't normally contain the entire story unless there are very strong emotions attached to the data chunk and it is strong enough to overcome the subconscious threshold to become part of our waking reality.

As we grow from birth to age five, we are like new sponges eager to absorb everything whether it comes from us or not. Humans become emotionally imprinted by our family of origin which usually consists of parents and siblings. We also learn certain coping behaviors that become part of the reaction matrix stored in the subconscious template of our physical brains. The developing brain is hardwired to free itself so that it can notice changes. The brain does this by reducing the learned behaviors into subconscious habits. Then, as we are confronted with similar situations later in life, the brain will react with the preprogrammed habit from our emotional slate developed between the ages of zero to five. This sets the stage for evolving consciousness. Humans are different from animals because the human brain is flexible enough to consciously change the habits once we can identify better and more productive behaviors.

Love and relationships are knowing not with our mind, but with our heart. Emotional IQ counts for much more in our society than intellectual IQ (see *Emotional Intelligence: Why It Can Matter More Than IQ*, by Daniel Goleman). In fact, people who know how to empathize and communicate with others on an emotional level are far more successful in life than people who are brilliant but have no socialization skills. The Dalai Lama, in *Destructive Emotions: A Scientific Dialogue with the Dalai Lama*, directly ties meditation and positive thoughts to rerouting the brain pathways to connect with spirit more easily. Our natural spiritual state is one of pure love.

One of the greatest gifts that we have is the freedom of choice. We can choose to exist as products of our physical brain, or we can choose to evolve by being one with spirit by mastering our emotions. Knowing ourselves through the lens of our emotions is the key to evolving consciousness. We can make conscious decisions to change our preprogrammed behaviors and overcome our negative, animal emotions. As evolving *Homo sapiens*, we have the ability to be more than just our brain; we can reconcile with our spiritual self by bringing that spiritual love into our dualistic bodies here on earth.

EARTHLY BODIES

Being human means all of us are made of heaven and earth. We have certain needs, certain wants, and are hardwired to notice change and to interpret our world in an orderly, habitual fashion. These are our human attributes that make us like animals and enforce our pack mentality. I know these statements are probably not what you want to read at this point, but it is vital to understand the dichotomy of body and soul in order to understand relationships and how to make the most of our earthly existence.

I'm sure most of you are familiar with the food groups. You have a food pyramid, and you follow it as a way to ensure proper eating for optimum health. Similarly, Maslow had an interesting way of looking at the world by categorizing people's needs in a pyramid-type of hierarchy. He categorized these needs as basic human needs. As they become fulfilled, a person is able to exercise higher cognitive functions like altruism. Self-actualization and helping others are the highest human expressions we can reach in our earthly bodies.

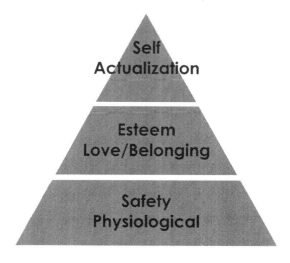

On the bottom of the pyramid are physical needs like breathing, food, water, and sleep. Then comes shelter and comfort, which encompasses being able to take care of oneself. Next are love, family, and social acceptance. Then the person evolves to concentrate on respect and self-esteem. Lastly, the person becomes a self-actualizer. At this stage of growth, the person can problem-solve and become concerned with helping others. Maslow said that a person couldn't function at a higher level of the pyramid unless the lower parts of the need pyramid were fulfilled first. Conversely, if a person moves to a higher need, like helping others, and then loses a primal need, such as food or shelter, he or she will temporarily go back and fix the primal needs first before continuing on to higher goals like helping others.

One can argue that this model is not entirely accurate. When people live in poverty, they still can and do help one another in ways such as sharing food or looking out for one another. However, I like Maslow's model because, despite its technical inaccuracy, the "hierarchy of needs" shows us what it is to be human. We are very similar to animals when we are clothed with the body of humanness. Just like animals, we need physical food and shelter, emotional love and acceptance, and mental stimulation so we don't become bored and listless.

Some understanding of the subconscious is highly relevant to a discussion of soulmates. In many ways the subconscious can be likened to a sixth sense. Some people notice messages from the subconscious more readily than other people. This subtle "knowing" by some people is also recognized as a root for empathy or intuition.

Because of the way humans evolved, about 95% of our behaviors are dictated by habit. We, as a species, only exercise our will or free choice in about 5% of the situations with which we are presented. Most of the time humans will react in a predictable pattern based on learned methods of coping. Primarily these coping mechanisms are learned from the ages of zero to five.

Have you ever heard why mothers cry at their daughters' weddings? The answer to the joke is, "Because the groom is so much like the father." Not to be cheeky, but there is a lot of truth in the joke. Most people will marry (at least the first time) someone that reminds them of their home life. They look to recreate the familiar; in other words, they look to create a situation that reinforces their habits. They will usually find it within models of behavior learned and observed from and between parents and/or siblings. There are strong reasons why adults may argue like children. Consequently, because of coping mechanisms learned as a child, it is not surprising to watch grown-up couples argue like two five-year-olds. This usually happens about issues that came into being when they were growing up and in ways they won arguments as five-year-olds.

Another aspect of being made of earth is that to survive, we follow the rules of society. Many times these rules reinforce a social hierarchy. To maintain order, there usually is a dominant person who enforces the social hierarchy. We unconsciously maintain this order because it is part of our evolutionary behavior habits. Another way to put it is that as humans, we follow energy. To survive, we notice those of greater and lesser energy. We have leaders and we have followers—shepherds and sheep.

Sound a little pack-like? Like wolves or canines? Cesar Millan has helped to raise awareness for our "best friends," the dogs. What is very interesting is that if you apply the "pack leader" mentality, it works on humans, too. When you are training your dog and your dog respects you, this is a calm assertive energy for the human and a calm submissive energy for the dog. People have this underlying structure of a pack in order to survive. The reason I mention this is because energy is very important in relationships. Understanding pack mentality is also a key to understanding the difference between being an animal and being human. It is that 5% of nonhabitual behavior that is the most interesting. That is the part of behavior that separates us from animals. That is the part that interfaces with the divine.

HEAVENLY BODIES

What is the divine? There are many answers depending on your viewpoint and cultural upbringing. Many people would consider that the divine is the same as the spiritual. Some might consider that the divine is an essence with which we try to merge. And still others may not think anything is divine if it doesn't relate to earth and earthly pleasures. It only makes sense that in order to understand "soul" mates, you have to delve into issues of the "soul."

My definition of "spiritual," after extensive study, is those actions that bring us closer to God. The divine is pure love, so those behaviors and actions that we exercise in the spirit of love are divine. Keep in mind there is a difference between spiritual and religious. I am talking about love and how to interact with others in the spirit of love. This is contrasted with the earthly bodies that act out of habit and Maslow's primal concerns noted above. In order to act out of love, we must transcend our earthly selves to exercise free will and choose to act with compassion. Then we interact with the divine. To understand more about the earthly world, our purpose on earth, and how to be in a soulmate relationship, near-death experiences (NDEs) have a lot of wisdom.

PART I: NDE WISDOM

KATE'S RAFTING EXPERIENCE–
A NEAR DEATH EXPERIENCE

It was a beautiful May day in sunny New Mexico. Kate was going on a whitewater rafting expedition she had signed up for in the small tourist town of Taos.

Wow! she thought when she woke up. *I've never gone rafting before and I'm really excited!* She quickly put on her shorts and T-shirt and heaped on the sunscreen. She stopped at the cute little shop called The Bean and was on her way with coffee and a portable bagel breakfast. The directions weren't that great, but she figured there was only one main road out of the town, so how bad could that be?

As she was taking in the breathtaking scenery of the river nestled between the mountains, she was also trying to stay on the winding road and eat at the same time. Such multitasking while looking for the river rafting place led her to doubt the directions. She fatefully pulled into the first rafting spot, not knowing it was not the one where she was signed up. When she parked the car and sauntered across the road, she went into the quaint shop. The gal behind the counter looked for Kate's reservation, but couldn't find it. Kate went back to the car to get her purse out of the trunk so she could get her credit card. She signed up again, not realizing that there were two rafting services and she was actually paying for two trips. But, as fate would have it, this was a universal coincidence she wouldn't understand until several days later. Kate returned to the car to put her purse away.

When she got back, people were loading into the van that was pulling the rafting boats. She quickly got in the van and fastened her seatbelt. After driving for several miles, the van pulled over onto a side road next to the river. Everyone got out and waited for the rafting guides to get the rafts into the water. In the meantime, other guides were explaining to the group what to expect, the stop off for lunch, and most importantly how to row, when to row, and safety measures in case the raft tipped over. The one thing that she remembered out of the talk was to keep your toes pointed downstream so you don't get caught in something from the bottom of the river. Then the guides doled out the life vests and made sure they were tightly wrapped and properly buckled on each person.

The river was still fairly high from the spring melt-off from the mountains. The city, hay season, and other drains on the river had not started to reduce the water flow. As a result, the river didn't have quite as many rapids since the rocks were still covered by water. Yet when there was white water, it was faster, deeper, and more dangerous than at other times of the year.

There were three boats to choose from. Kate didn't know anyone. The other members of the group seemed to come in pairs or in families. So she positioned herself to be in a boat not filled with children. The boat she would be on held a newlywed couple, a leftover man from one of the family excursions, and the guide. That meant that one person was up front. The person who gravitated to the lead spot was the leftover man. Then the couple, who were both on the heavyset side, got in on the next seat. Kate went to the left side without a balancing partner. The guide took the back center position. The boat was a little off-balance, but as long as the newlywed man stayed on the left side, it wasn't a bad arrangement. Then it was time to take off after the other two rafts. Kate's raft brought up the rear.

Floating was nice. Dip, pull, float a little more. Beautiful scenery! It was almost easier to sit and watch the birds go by. But then the silence would be interrupted by another command from the guide, "Row left." So Kate paddled since she was on the left side.

The first rapids were fairly small. With a little paddling at the right time, the raft did a little dip-de-dip, a little water came in, but nothing scary or hard to handle. This gave all of the first-timers some confidence, a little adrenaline, and big smiles. This procedure was repeated about four times. Everyone was feeling good, and this was a great trip.

Then came the next set of rapids. These rapids were longer and had higher white water than what the group had experienced so far. But they had confidence in each other and in the directions of their guide to make it through the rapids again. The raft picked up speed and hit the choppy water. It bobbed up and down as the guide yelled, "Row right, hard right!" Kate could see the rock they were heading for, and her eyes got big, but that determination to avoid disaster spurred her to shove that paddle into the torrid water and hold steady. The combined efforts of the boaters easily helped the raft into the eddy before the final push out of the rapids. The guide asked everyone how they were doing. With the high five of the paddles clacking together, the group glided into the rapids again. They shot through with a couple of paddle strokes into the relatively calm water. The rest of the group was waiting. The guides had a favorite rock where they took groups "surfing." The first two groups, even the children, paddled back upstream to the rock where they shot back down the river backwards.

It was Kate's group's turn. They paddled up-stream to the rock but overshot it a bit, causing the boat to tip up to the right side. The raft was destabilized, gave a couple of attempts to right itself, and then lost it, depositing everyone, including the guide, into the torrid waters. In that moment, all Kate could do was think, *Oh, shit, oh shit, oh shit! Is this really happening? Is the raft really flipping?* As she hit the cold water and went under, the survival adrenaline came rushing through her veins. All she could remember was to keep her toes pointed downstream to keep from getting caught in the hidden, deadly tree roots or rocks on the bottom of the river. But unfortunately, the life vest got snagged on a tree root and she couldn't get free. She desperately tried to get to the top of the rapids, but was so disoriented, she couldn't figure out which way was up. Being in the tight grip of the root, it wouldn't have mattered anyway. She needed desperately to breath, but was surrounded by the chaotic, torrid water. She tried to right herself, but the current was too strong. She was tiring fast. As she was running out of air, it all seemed hopeless. She stopped struggling and went limp. She was drowning, and there was nothing she could do about it. She surrendered and was silently praying that God was there.

At that moment, she separated from her body. She was looking down on the chaos and could see her raft partners in various stages of getting back into the raft. She could also vaguely hear the other two raft guides yelling to find her. But strangely, it didn't matter. She was so happy and relaxed. Kate then saw a bright light. She was captivated by the warmth. She wanted to get a closer look.

That decision flung her through a tunnel and simultaneously a life review. How could that be? She had her life flash before her eyes in a panoramic view. One particular experience she had forgotten had to do with one stressful moment where she snapped at her sister for something that her sister didn't do. Kate actually felt the agony she had caused her sister in that moment and saw a ripple effect as the anger and pain affected her sister's children, her sister's husband, and her sister's co-workers. Kate was very moved and ashamed. Kate saw and felt the gratitude of the shabbily dressed little girl who was longingly looking at the ice cream truck that stopped to sell ice cream to all the neighborhood children. Kate didn't realize it, but her act of kindness to this little girl of giving her money for the ice cream cone had far-reaching consequences in that little one's life. Who knew the effect of one random act of kindness? In a split second, Kate resolved she would do better. She realized that her words had the power to heal or to harm.

After the life review, Kate found herself walking in the light. She had overwhelming feelings of love, peace, and joy. These feelings were so intense that they were indescribable, like nothing she had ever experienced on earth. Next she saw her beloved grandmother. Her grandmother had wasted away to ninety pounds with the cancer. She was so weak and frail when she died. Yet, here she was, a healthy one hundred and fifty pounds—radiating health and life.

"Grandma, is that you?" asked Kate. Kate was a bit surprised that even though she was thinking this, the words didn't come out of her mouth.

Her grandmother telepathically replied, "Yes, Kate, it is me. I have permission to show you around a little bit, but it is not your time. You will need to return to earth."

Kate was surprised to hear this in her head. She mused, *So this is what telepathy is like.* She then said, "Grandma, I have really missed you. I miss going fishing. I miss being able to laugh with you and play cribbage."

Kate's grandmother came over and gave her a big hug, "Yes, dear, I have missed you, too. But you need to realize that I am always with you. I am very happy here and know that it won't be long before we are reunited again. We don't view time like you do."

"Grandma, are we in heaven?" asked Kate.

Smiling, Grandma laughed and said, "Heaven? I suppose you could call it that. It is a beautiful place that radiates God's love. We still have jobs, and we still learn. I would call it a level of heaven."

As she floated away from the mouth of the tunnel, Grandma asked her, "Let's have tea in the garden, shall we?" Kate instantly floated past a group of people in a line. It looked like they were coming back to earth.

Kate asked, "Are those people being reincarnated?"

"Yes, but not quite in the way you expect," answered Grandma. "These people are in line to look through the lens of infinite possibilities and then, after choosing their lessons they want to experience, they are assigned a body, and only then are they allowed to incarnate on earth in the particular possibility of their choosing. Sometimes they have guides help them choose; other times it is totally up to the individual soul."

Just then they stopped in the most beautiful garden Kate had ever seen. It reminded her of the British estates with flowers, labyrinths, and trees set forth in a spectacular design that was totally awe-inspiring. There were no colors like it on earth. Everything was alive and covered with an extra glow of light; the grass, the flowers, the trees. Even the stream sang as it gurgled by.

The talk with Kate's grandmother seemed to last forever, yet in reality, only lasted for minutes. Grandma explained the mysteries of the universe and even talked of some of the lessons for which Kate needed to return to earth. Kate's grandmother was grinning when she introduced Kate to her future son. Kate was speechless. What a gorgeous little boy with red hair, bright blue eyes, and freckles—lots of them! She did manage to gather her wits around to ask him if he could give her a sign so she would be able to know that it was him when he was born. He then pointed to a patch of red on his right forearm. He told her that he would carry that into his earthly life, and she would know it was him by this sign.

After Kate had finished her favorite Irish tea with her grandmother, Grandma said, "It is time now, sweetie. You need to go back now. Remember, I'll be with you always."

Boom! She felt like toothpaste being squished into a tube. She was back in her body. Choke, sputter! Cough. Kate exhaled water and took in a deep life-sustaining breath. She was back. But what about Grandma? Where was she?

As Kate gained consciousness, she saw the ambulance and realized that the paramedics had brought her back to life. She heard one say, "I thought you were a goner. I didn't think you were coming back."

"How, long?" rasped Kate, as she managed to exhale and barely vibrate the vocal cords.

"You've been gone about thirty minutes," replied the paramedic.

THE NEAR-DEATH EXPERIENCE

Kate had a near-death experience (NDE). A lot of my world view is based upon consciousness studies. For the past decade, I have been the webmaster of three websites devoted to the study of different aspects of consciousness for the past decade. Each of the three websites, www.nderf.org, www.adcrf.org, and www.oberf.org, asks people to fill out a survey form about their experience. The study participant answers the questions and provides narratives describing his or her experience. These answers are analyzed to determine characteristics of different states of consciousness. Most experiences are categorized and posted on the relevant website.

There are many books about consciousness. The one model of consciousness that makes the most sense given the data from NDEs is that we have a body and that our consciousness survives bodily death. Rene Descartes, who lived in the early 1600s, is considered the father of philosophy. One of his theories had to do with dualism. Descartes talked about dualism as body and mind, with "mind" being synonymous with soul. I will usually use the term "consciousness," because the word "soul" is such a loaded, religious term. Essentially, by changing the terms of the study, it is easier to objectively understand consciousness.

The Near-Death Experience Research Foundation (NDERF) website has an amazing collection of articles. Since 1999, we have about 2,400 experiences that are NDEs, probable NDEs, or possible NDEs.

NDERF focuses on studying the state of consciousness when a person has an experience while physically dead or during an imminently life-threatening event. During this unique state of consciousness, it is physically impossible, or "medically inexplicable," to have a lucid experience apart from the body when the brain is dead, unconscious, or under certain types of anesthesia. Hence, this simplification provides the underlying rationale for the validity of consciousness outside of the body and the reality of the afterlife.

NDERF is the largest website of its kind in the world and bounces between number one and number three on the various Web search engines. This occurred from popular search interest of people wanting to know more about NDEs and not because of paying for the ranking. What makes NDERF unique is that it has a global outreach of over twenty languages and provides the means to study NDE phenomena throughout the world.

For more information about the near-death experience written with scientific rigor, I would highly recommend reading *Evidence of the Afterlife: The Science of Near-Death Experiences*, by Jeffrey Long, M.D. The soulmates book springboards from but does not reiterate the findings of *Evidence of the Afterlife*. Rather, this book concentrates on the way that people change after they have a NDE and their unique perspectives on love and relationships. It is the spiritual content that I find so compelling.

When I was working with Jeff on *Evidence of the Afterlife*, we started to analyze the narrative content and the answers from the NDERF Web form survey asking questions of NDErs about their near-death experience. The content review project is unique in that all experiences posted on the website, regardless of whether they answered questions or not, are included in the study. What we found was that there was more than enough evidence for the afterlife. But I found that proving the afterlife was not as interesting to me as the spiritual and emotional content that the NDErs shared with us. The NDE answers provided guidance as to how to live our lives based on the greater reality and evidence from heaven. In my opinion, proving the afterlife is a mental exercise to satisfy scientists, skeptics, and atheists. It has to be done to help validate the near-death experience to the world as a real experience. But the real importance of the content review study is to provide guidance on how to best live life on earth so we can enjoy that afterlife. In other words, what is our purpose on earth, and how do we help our consciousness to grow so we can enjoy the afterlife?

Having incontrovertible evidence of the afterlife is a pretty bold claim, so the substantiation process is fairly rigorous. There are an average number of 750 consecutive experiences that are analyzed—and I give Lynn Russell heartfelt thanks for her help in this enormous project! With such a large sample of people, there emerges a consensus on certain concepts. These concepts are so powerful that they then become the basis for changes of behavior. For instance, if one of the biggest human phobias is the fear of death, then how do people change their behaviors on earth if they realize they are immortal? Or how do people change with respect to their relationships when they realize that the other side is pure love, times a million?

Some of the NDE wisdom are simple concepts that we all know, such as "love God" and "love your neighbor." However, there are other concepts that are less well-known but still every bit as important to our purpose on earth.

One lesser-known concept is that encounters with the light are equated by many NDErs as encounters with God or heaven. Many times NDErs describe God, love, and light as the same concept, all rolled into one visual and emotional package. The nature of God or heaven is so overwhelmingly potent and synonymous with such love and feelings of heaven as the true home, that it makes it impossible to accurately put into words. We can only approximate descriptions of the love and homecoming that NDErs experience. If we actually can understand what love is and the true nature of a living God, then that changes behaviors and the way we interact with others on earth—for the better.

The continuity of life is another life-changing concept. Many people come back with the concept of reincarnation. Others come back with wonderful descriptions of heaven. Very few encountered hell or scary afterlives. But as Barbara Rommer discussed in her book *Blessings in Disguise*, even these less-than-positive NDEs have spiritual silver linings. These NDErs drastically changed the way they lived on earth to avoid returning to unpleasant hereafters. Some of the changes that people report based upon the continuity of life were that they concentrated more on family, relationships, and helping others, and less on monetary gain. They approached life with purpose and were more accepting of earthly lessons. Importantly, they didn't live life in fear or with guilt.

Another area that changed the NDEr the most was whether or not the NDE was consistent with his or her attitudes or belief system prior to the experience. Most people focused on the change in their religious/spiritual practices. In the NDERF study, there is a difference between "religious" and "spiritual." "Religion" refers to organized religion. In this book, my definition of "spiritual" refers to all actions that lead one closer to God. The most interesting change was when NDErs get the epiphany that God is real. We have so many religions that talk about faith, but to transition to the conviction that "God is real" is a powerful concept that speaks to the failures of religion and the hope for mankind. The largest upshot of realizing God is *real* is that this caused people to change the way they practiced their religion and the way they treated others on earth. Many lost their fear of being judged or feeling guilty and started living by helping others. They started to practice love, not just talk about it in church.

I have teased you a little bit with some of the findings. For many, these statements may seem like a "duh" or "OMG" moment. But others want to see more substantiation of such sweeping conclusions. I'm going to not only talk about these concepts and how they came into being, but also start setting the stage for the rest of the book. The NDE concepts provide the baseline to measure soulmate relationships—how to find one and how to transform yourself within that relationship. The journey is our purpose on earth—to learn about love. We do this by doing loving acts towards ourselves and others.

Concepts from the NDErs' answers will be discussed. These concepts are of love, light and religious beings. Then I will explore their answers concerning earthly relationships. The next section talks about motivators that help us evolve into better people. And lastly, I think it is important to explore issues that I categorize as the "human condition." Issues of duality in the human condition are those issues we wrestle with every day, such as fear and empowerment, sin and forgiveness, goodness and evil.

CONCEPTS REGARDING LOVE, THE LIGHT, AND RELIGIOUS BEINGS

Love: "Gotta get me some more of dat!"

The messages that most NDErs talk about have to do with love. Love is the glue that holds the universe together; it is God, light, the unity of all, and ultimately what we separate from to be born on earth. Love is what we strive to achieve on earth. We are created in God's image of pure love. We are that spark of being, that cell of life incarnated on earth from the universal "All." Paradoxically, our fragmentation from universal love to come to earth is what motivates us to keep trying to be reunited with that love. That is what makes us uniquely human. We are subjected to a realm of dualities to forge our individual character so that we can become stronger when we reunite with God.

Although love is the goal, it is one of the hardest concepts to describe; especially the intensity with which it is felt during the NDE. So one of the ways that we can explore love is to understand what it is like and what it is not like. Love can be described in combination with other qualities. It has modifier language that can give more meaning to the word "love." Finally, people compare love to something they are familiar with on earth.

The one quality that outshines all when referencing "love" is peace. Love and peace go together in the same sentence more often than any other words. Next are concepts of warmth, joy, happiness, ecstasy, indescribability, compassion, acceptance, calmness, being complete or fullness, comfort, beauty, purity, eternity, security, no fear, forgiveness, safety, not of this world, goodness, and truth.

Love stronger than anything really exists but it can't be described with our words... Our task is to hand over this love around us. (Bardin's NDE)

The light, This Most Holy Spirit, took me into itself, in an embrace that will haunt me to the end of my days and beyond. For an endless instant I knew Love. And I knew myself loved beyond words and descriptions. Just infinitely loved. (Herbert's NDE)

It is hard to communicate the incredible feeling of peace and love that seemed to envelop me, making me feel worthwhile, loved etc. (Tawnie's NDE)

The light radiated love and peace. I wanted to experience it and be in its presence. (Scott's NDE)

The major descriptors NDErs used to describe love are "overwhelming," "deep," "incredible," "profound," "supreme," "awe-inspiring," "strong," "extreme," "intense," and "wonderful."

Every need, want, and desire was supplied by the all powerful force of Love. This Love

*was so powerful, so extremely fulfilling—
everything else was immaterial...full of loving peace...Supreme Love flooded me.
(Ron's NDE)*

*There was an overwhelming sense of love,
to where nothing in the world could even
come close to. (Patricia's NDE)*

*I looked at the light and I experienced an
overwhelming flood of peace, joy, and
unconditional love. (Nellie's NDE)*

The number one concept to emerge is love
as a lesson or purpose on earth. Not surprisingly,
"unconditional love" and "surrounded" or "em-
braced" by love were the next two concepts. The
next highest ranked concept was that love, light,
and God are the same. Most people reported
becoming more loving after the NDE. Some
equated this love to being more loving of their
family, friends, and humanity in general. Several
people said that the love felt so good that they
didn't want to leave heaven and come back to
earth. Many times it is the love and the separation from love that causes the anger or longing
to return to heaven that is typical among NDErs.
Here are a few of their comments:

*I had a small taste of the awesome love
and perfect peace of God. There is no
fear in love, but perfect love casts out fear.
God is love, and God loves us more than
we can possibly imagine. (Roger's NDE)*

They made this reverberating love feeling like the ripple effect when someone throws a stone into water, but this was love, not water. It sprinkled down onto you and is the single greatest type of love that I have ever experienced. (Bryan's NDE)

I felt completely loved. Worst part is feeling separated from the love. (Shawna's NDE)

Sometimes people would try to describe love in terms of what they knew. Some people equated love to be like a first kiss. Some equated love to the bond between mother and child. Several said that they were cradled or sitting on the lap of God or Jesus.

I looked around and realized I was sitting on a man's lap, who was dressed in white robes. . . I knew it was Jesus. (Mary's NDE)

After reviewing what the NDErs said, it is a simple message that we hear over and over again—Love is the most important thing, and love is all there is. But don't take my word for it, read it yourself directly from the NDErs:

I learned that the only thing in life is unconditional love. (Lloyd 's NDE)

He told me very clearly, "It's all about love." (Ann Marie's NDE)

I know now that what really matters is how much you love people and how much you are loved by people in life. (Jo's NDE)

My whole life changed. I am relaxed about life, have been able to deal with experiences with love as the focus, and I'm not afraid of anything. There is a peace and a gentleness, a love and a compassion that was born in me that night of the accident. (Michelle's NDE)

What is meaningful to me is that death is simple and that the love we experience here on earth is magnified a hundred times over, and that, my friend, is a beautiful feeling. (Jo's NDE)

Love was all that mattered. (Kami's NDE)

Love is a power that knows no boundary, even in death. (Timothy's NDE)

I remember that love and knowledge are all that really matter in life. (Darlene's NDE)

Love-being loved—loving back—LOVE was all there is. (Barbara's NDE)

I sent love from my heart to the other souls. I felt at least 10,000 other hearts return that love to me. (Denny's NDE)

The feeling coming from this energy was pure unconditional love. It was beyond human love, a love so tremendously great that the English language does not do justice to explain what I felt. (Lindsey's NDE)

All these descriptions and qualities about love show it is extremely important to us, or at least it should be extremely important to us as humans. But are these descriptions enough for non-NDErs to understand an emotion that we have only a small taste of on earth? Would we truly recognize what love is, or is our conception of love skewed by the harsh reality of daily life and with a healthy dose of how the media portrays love? And for those who have found love, how do we make love more powerful than the negative earthly emotions of hate, anger, and despair? Do we know love when we see it? Here are a few more concepts that can help us to better understand love.

THE LIGHT

One of the main concepts that describes or directly relates to love is "the light." As I went through the narratives about light, it became clear that there were many categories and descriptors that one could use regarding it. Light is one of the most common elements of the NDE. It is also the most difficult to analyze because descriptions of light show the cultural or educational choices of language as well as its limitations.

One person could describe the light as a magnificent, brilliant light. Another could describe the same light as a bright white light, while yet another could describe it as simply a "light."

Another example is if you, the reader, and I see the same light, we may describe it very differently because we are different people with different ways of communicating. What is important to me may not be important to you. I may describe the visual intensity of bright light, yet you might concentrate on the feelings that light invokes within you. Both descriptions are entirely accurate, yet there are many ways to perceive and express what people see or feel about one event.

Descriptors include the light as a place, going to the light, being surrounded by light, the location of the light, the color, its relationship to the tunnel element of the NDE, emotions, many descriptions of what the light looked like, what qualities light has, whether the light is human or a being, if the light has intelligence, light as in weight, light as in travel, and contrasting light with dark.

Another viewpoint of light can be seen when NDErs describe the out-of-body (OBE) phase of the NDE. After experiencers have a life-threatening event, they may transition out of their body and still be able to experience earthly events. The experiencer may describe tubes of light or light as a method of travel, such as floating up in a light. They may describe the operating room light, a shaft of light, or a "zap" of white light. Light described during the OBE phase is most likely the closest to describing what we know of earthly light and, therefore, the easiest for NDErs to communicate to others.

> *I found myself on the dark side of the light. There was a barrier of lace, and on the other side it was so warm and bright. (Carol's NDE)*

> *Both light and darkness, but not like either, unseparated without shadow. (Anaica's NDE)*

> *How can I define what is positive in darkness? Well, positive is light. Then, suddenly, I was in light; bright, white, shiny, and strong; a very bright light. It was like the flash of a camera, but not flickering—that bright. (George's NDE)*

Most people have heard of the light at the end of the tunnel, and it does turn out to be the most mentioned description. Many people do see light in the tunnel and some may describe the tunnel as like a tube of light. Some say that the colors are rainbow, blue, yellow, or green. Many times when describing light in the tunnel, it is because there is a being of light in the tunnel with the experiencer.

> *Then I entered a yellow light tunnel. The tunnel had a ring structure and my hand would not pass through wall. I traveled down the center of the tunnel until I touched the*

wall at high speed which made me crash into the walls until I regained equilibrium. I heard a voice saying words of encouragement like, "You mustn't worry . . . dying is easy . . . you're nearly there." The tunnel opened outwards, like the end of a trumpet, into a space like a sky with rainbow colors. (Anne's NDE)

The tunnel appears to be evidential of the co-creation theory of the NDE. Both the experiencer and the divine create the experience in the most loving way possible for the NDErs to maximize living their life for when they come back to earth. As a loving creator could attest, a tunnel could be necessary to ease the transition from earth to the divine. Few people who experienced light while _in_ the tunnel said that they were drawn to the light or that they were sucked through the tunnel. This implies that there is some choice and free will in going to the light. However, there aren't any experiences that say that the experiencer in the tunnel turned back. They did go forward to the light.

The tunnel had a white brightness or rays leading to the end of the tunnel and to a warm, more yellow light. (Lavona's NDE)

I was walking down a HUGE yellow tunnel which seems to be made of yellow glass or light, the whole thing is glowing. It's like being in something the size of an airplane

*hanger, only taller, and as I mentioned it is
a great big tunnel. (Amber's NDE)*

Some of the most intriguing descriptions are
those that have to do with light after the NDEr
goes through the tunnel. Many times the NDEr
describes light as a place to go to or a bright
room. The descriptions can be likened to what we
imagine heaven to be like. This is a place where
we and all things in heaven are filled with and
emanating light. The light is commonly described
as the place to "go to" or the direction in which
we should move. Many talk about merging with
the light, as if we are a part of a cosmic union of
souls. Others describe light cities and a river of
light. And still others liken the light to "home" and
"life itself."

*I was about to enter the light. I knew that I
was part of the light…Yes, it was like a road
of very white light, very pure when enter-
ing it; limitless happiness; at the end there
was an "inner circle" of very bright light.
(Pietro's NDE)*

*An infinite expanse of glorious light envel-
oped and permeated everything. This light
was evenly distributed and seemed to un-
dulate gently with a force field. (Ron's NDE)*

*Standing at the light, that is not really a light
like we know on earth, I felt I finally was home
after a long, long journey. (Shirley's NDE)*

Just this loving, ever loving Light! I'm home! I feel the unbelievable warmth, love, joy, and completeness of the Light! (Andrew's NDE)

Not surprisingly, white was the most common color of light. Blue was the next mentioned color, closely followed by gold, then silver. Several people described sparkling clear, crystal light, full spectrum light, or rainbow lights. Many people described colors that are not of this earth that they have never seen before.

I opened my eyes to a blinding white light. Everything was bright white. (Beth's NDE)

I came into a white light and in the distance it was pink and gold, like a sunrise. (Annie's NDE)

At first, the light was blue. Then it transitioned to white. It was an opalescent white; it almost glowed, but did not shine. It was bright, but not intense bright, like glowing bright - pure bright. (Anthony's NDE)

There were many descriptors of what the light looked like. The most common description is a bright light. Many called the bright light brilliant, beautiful, wonderful, magnificent, illuminating, tremendous, great, incredible, intense, beautiful, radiant, soft, glowing, clean, and pure. When trying to relate the bright light to what we know of earth, many said that the light was like the sun, the moon, the stars, rays, beams, a spotlight, a globe, spirals, luminous arcs, and a pinpoint of light that got bigger as the experiencer got closer. Another popular description was a bright light shining through trees, fog, water, or clouds.

I could see bright light, and in the light there were little lights coming at me. As they got closer they got bigger, and when they got to me they exploded into something that I can't explain. (Benjamin's NDE)

At this moment a piercing white beam of light the width of a pen shot down to us... The light was literally blinding, but I could stare directly into it without flinching...The light was getting brighter at this time, and wider. (Jedraine's NDE)

Most people are drawn to the light, but once in a while the light comes to them. One common theme was the NDErs' surprise that the light was so intensely bright, yet it didn't hurt their eyes. Only a few could not look at the light or needed time to get accustomed to the brightness. Some mentioned that the light was so bright that there were no shadows.

I saw a bright white light that doesn't hurt your eyes. I was drawn to it, like I had to go to it - kind of magnetic. (Mel's NDE)

The light was bright but not blazing to hurt your eyes. The light had an energy that drew me near and made me want to enter it above all else. It was obviously a gate-way to a place where I felt a strong need to go. (Kristin's NDE)

Even though the location of the light was seldom mentioned, the most common directions were up or coming from within or behind relatives or other beings. There were several mentions of the light coming from behind or from an open door or light connected with a boundary. The NDErs describe knowing that if they cross through the door or go through the light, they would not be able to come back to their earthly body. Interestingly, light was also used in connection with travel.

I entered into an arc of light. It was like traveling through thousands of luminous arcs, extremely beautiful; their radiance seemed to increase during the time I traveled through them. (Alejandro's NDE)

Many times the light would either emanate an emotion or it would evoke an emotion in the NDEr. The most mentioned emotion connected to the light was unconditional love. Many said the light was calming, peaceful, gave immense joy, limitless happiness and euphoria, and that the light was soft, comforting, safe, and warm. These descriptors are exactly what we long for in our relationships, and it is comforting to know that they will be on the other side for us to fully experience. This sounds like a homecoming and just what one would imagine heaven to be like.

And then a bright light came around me and it felt as though the light became a large hand that surrounded and cradled me in it with warmth and comfort. (Mari's NDE)

I did experience an intense ray of light that wrapped itself around me. It felt so incredibly warm and comforting. (Roberta's NDE)

Some of my favorite parts of the light are those in connections with beings. There are numerous references to light beings, God as light, or light radiating from within deceased relatives. The light is also described as a living consciousness with total knowledge. Many experiencers describe themselves as having bodies of light during their NDE.

His face was bright and radiating like the sun with rays extending outward. There was no face, but pure light. I could look straight into the bright light of his face and it didn't hurt my eyes. (Lizzette's NDE)

modes, coming down from the mt. w/the 10 Commandments

There was one major being of love and many other beings of love with actual personhood or souls. I could not see much but light and vague outlines in a way. There was nothing but love, goodness, truth, and all things to do with love with NO ROOM for fear or evil or anything but this love. It was more wonderful than any of my best hopes or experiences on this planet. It was beyond perfect and loving as we in our human state know it. No words to describe it. (Veronica's NDE)

The light emanated from the presence in the void and was unworldly in its brilliance and purity, and it faded as I left the void and went back. (Kim's NDE)

I don't know if it was light or spiritual/ natural energy; it was holy. (Bruce's NDE)

According to the NDErs, many talk about a universal connection that is being or becoming one with God, the light, the universe, and everyone and everything. Several mention that we are all fragmented sparks of God who come to earth as individuals, but then upon death, we are rejoined or reconnected to the collective, infinite whole. This is interesting because those experiencing a frightening NDE rarely feel like they are a part of the collective, but instead report being separated from God, fragmented, and fearful. Becoming part of the whole is to experience love, peace, knowledge, harmony, and union. Love is the glue that holds everything together in a common bond of unity.

I lifted up the skin of Creation, and saw that every living thing in Creation was an expression of this being, connected to this being, indivisible and of One. Every person, plant, animal, insect, microbe, drew its very existence from this Being. (Dan's NDE)

We are all a part of God, like a cell in our bloodstream. Our connection to each other and our only way to return to the ONE is Love. Without LOVE, we cannot communicate with each other, much less with God. (Gail's NDE)

I felt and learned that we are all connected together...everything... a huge matrix of universal substance and being...Every individual thing is a piece of it, single cells within forever. (Gregg's NDE)

There are also concepts of what it means on earth to be universally connected to everyone and everything. A core concept is one of accountability for our individual actions. Every action causes reactions in everyone and everything, much like a planetary ripple effect. This concept was also discussed above in relation to the life review. Many people report total knowledge on the other side, and secrets or hiding information is not possible because of the telepathy and total truth on the other side. On the other hand, others report that there are schools, halls of learning, and halls of healing. So, there is not total knowledge as we would perceive it here on earth. There is also a group consciousness or a collective-whole concept that emerges. Some of the group consciousness could account for the concept of soulmates—those people who are closely connected to each other for various lessons on earth.

I did not know the beings, but felt loved by them as if I was part of them. (Don's NDE)

Everyone that does evil things against neighbors or against God really is doing evil against oneself. (Peter's NDE)

I was told that I [as an individual] was incredibly special and that "we all" belong to one another, and that we are all responsible to one another and to all living things. (Tom's NDE)

My life had touched all the people in it— it was sort of like a tapestry and showed how I affected everyone's lives around me. (Anita's NDE)

I was also experiencing my every action as everyone affected by my actions. I could literally feel the concentric circles of "emotion" going out from me, as they were experienced by each person in turn. (Dan's NDE)

It seems almost ironic that we are so fragmented in our homes, society, and the world, yet we are so connected to everything and everybody. We just don't realize it here on earth.

CONCEPTS ABOUT RELIGIOUS BEINGS

I find it quite humbling to be in the position of trying to summarize and communicate these concepts of love, light, beauty, magnificence, etc. You almost can share the ecstatic experience of the NDEr in reading some of these accounts. I think distinct and separate concepts of "God," "Jesus," and "The Light" may not be altogether right. The concept of connection and the overlap in descriptions of these concepts is very evident. So I have chosen to put together the concepts of Love, Light, and Religious Beings.

Many NDErs describe God as light, love, all-knowing, and powerful. They often express feeling awe at being in the presence of God. Interestingly, God does not seem to identify himself as "God." NDErs often know or feel they are in the presence of God. Many describe the connection to God and the unity of all things to God. The feelings are so deep that many times NDErs communicate their encounter with God through intense poetic words. *Psalms* There are a few references to the classic appearance of God on a throne. God may appear with Jesus; the voice is beautiful. God may be communicating with the NDEr at the end of the experience about tasks to do and the NDEr's return to earthly life.

When a person encountered a being other than Jesus or God, he or she would most typically describe this person as a loving male being of light, like a spiritual guide. This person would radiate unconditional love, compassion, warmth, peace, knowledge, and acceptance, and would inspire love, happiness, joy, ecstasy, comfort, caring, and safety in the NDEr. Most of the time, this religious being was unknown to the experiencer. Many experienced only hearing a voice, while others were only cognizant of a presence without actually seeing the religious being. A few people described religious beings as a collective consciousness or as thousands of balls of lights.

That being was composed of love; it created love, it emitted love, it directed love. It lived on love. It was Love; Love the Power. There was nothing in that entire experience with the other Divine Loving Being that was not totally "good" and powered by "love". (DW's NDE)

Jesus was seen in various stages of his life. Many times he would be the baby Jesus with the Virgin Mary. Most of the time, Jesus was seen after Crucifixion. He was described various ways, with the most common description as a light being. One person described him as in his thirties, six feet tall, reddish brown hair, short beard and moustache. Several describe his robe or gown, ranging from the colors of white to golden beige and made of light, or being torn with a ragged hem. There were only a few people who saw Jesus on a thrown next to God. Many people described being in the arms, hands, or embrace of God or Jesus.

I met with a really awesome light being I understood to be Jesus. He took me into him and all I remember him saying was: Tell them to love one another. (David L. Oakfield's NDE)

The description of God had a lot more variability than religious beings. Several saw God in the shape of a person that may or may not have had a human face. Most of the people saw God as pure light, supreme energy, or the universal creative force. God may have appeared only as a voice or as a presence. There were only a few people who saw God seated on a throne.

Then I was in front of this being, looking at him. I knew he was holy. I felt this was God appearing to me as I had always imagined him. An old man with a large beard. He had taken on this persona so that I would not be afraid. (Lucia's NDE)

God is in every fiber of the universe. He's all over and knows all. He's not a person as some may think. God is an energy. (Ethyl's NDE)

Before my eyes, I saw all of Creation as in a crystal ball, floating in this grayness. Wrapped around Creation was a Being of stunning majesty, as if it grew from his body. (Dan's NDE)

His face was bright and radiating like the sun with rays extending outward. There was no face, but pure light. I could look straight into the bright light of his face and it didn't hurt my eyes. To the left and to the right of Him stood several beings like men standing at attention. I was in the presence of God, when I had no religious or biblical knowledge. (Lizette's NDE)

I asked it was it Jesus or Buddha or Mohammed? It said, "I am the light." (Francis's NDE)

Interestingly, many people have the option of co-creating their experience. This may indicate that the experiencer is allowed to see whom or what he or she wishes to see, and this may be a factor that makes the experience easier for the NDEr.

I remembered from my Sunday school classes that if a person asks to see the Lord, he shall see him. I asked to see Jesus. (John's NDE)

I asked her if I could speak to God. Then God came down. (Mary's NDE)

I decided to go back to my origin and the origin of everything, the Light. (Roger's NDE)

When you read the descriptions about love, the light, and religious beings, you can't escape the conclusion that this is an amazing concept. If we understood that love is the emotion that comes when you experience peace, joy, warmth, and security, it isn't surprising we would call that heaven. Being on earth, many times we experience the opposite of the description of love, yet most of us strive to become whole by reconnecting with love, the light, and God. NDErs have had the awesome experience of feeling that love, connection, and unity outside of their earthly body. They know it is out there and are special emissaries to help the rest of us remember where we come from and where we are returning.

CONCEPTS REGARDING EARTHLY RELATIONSHIPS

After looking at what NDErs were saying about relationships, there are a few categories that stuck out. The answers are grouped according to qualities, relationship dynamics, gratitude, purposes, and alienation. It is so important to understand what NDErs are saying about relationships. This is the way we express love. This is the *action* that allows us to reconnect with the greater reality of love, the light, and God. At the end of our earthly life, only those actions done of love are what matters. The more of these loving actions and relationships that we have, the more loving energy we are allowed to bring with us and, ultimately, the more connected and less fragmented we are in the afterlife.

The quality that stands head and shoulders above all other answers and groups is that NDErs "love more." Other qualities in order of appearance are that NDErs are more compassionate, forgiving and less judgmental, relaxed, tolerant, understanding, kinder, more caring, trying to be good people, more giving, patient, not afraid, better listeners, less concerned about what others think, less self-centered, less interested in material success, more involved with others, open-minded, more focused on unconditional love, humble, self-controlled, balanced, happier, and more concerned with treating others with respect.

We all need to reach out to others in love, finding little ways to let them know someone cares. On earth, it's we who must work at expressing the love that ultimately runs the universe. (Catherine's NDE)

The intensity of the love I have for those in my life is a thousand times greater. (Mark's NDE)

I serve instead of expecting to be served. I forgive and love and don't think the effort would have been made were it not for that experience and the knowledge that that's all that really matters. (Kami's NDE)

The only thing that matters is how your actions or words make another feel. (Kent's NDE)

The most important thing in life here is treating people right, being a good person, and showing love for others. (Maria's NDE)

In talking about relationship dynamics, most said that their relationships improved after their NDE. Their priorities, perspectives, and lives turned around. Many were closer to spouse, family, and friends, and more committed in their relationships. Others reported that their marriage ended in divorce or their current relationships got worse and their social circle changed. Even though these changes were initially harsh, ultimately they reflected a change for the better. The more altruistic changes had to do with a closer relationship to God and love for humanity.

> I was told that you are here to gain knowledge and to learn how to love. . . I realized that when the entity said "you" it didn't mean just me, it meant the human race. (Barbara's NDE)

> It really did give me a love for mankind, though, and all in all it made me who I am. I have a unique way of looking at life. I love mankind because I know what we gave up to come here. We have something to learn and evidently this life is the best place. (Nancy's NDE)

> I am more conscious of loving God and my neighbor. (Bruce's NDE)

There were many NDErs who talked about gratitude. They appreciate their families more, have gratitude for life, appreciate people, friends, children, and "everything."

Family and love are most important. (Denise's NDE)

I was a "work first then family" guy, but now I know that nothing is more important than family. (Steven's NDE)

There was a smaller proportion, but still a significant group of people, who had more problems relating to others after their NDE. They reported that they were more hypersensitive, so more reclusive and closed to others.

I do have greater difficulty relating to people who have not experienced this as I at times feel they may think I'm a bit "loopy" as I have different priorities. (Chrissie's NDE)

Several commented that their relationships with others were lessons or roles that they needed to learn or to play. Some went so far as to talk about the fact that life on earth is transitory, so they chose not to play anymore. Many people changed jobs so that they could be more giving and compassionate towards others.

For the rest of your earthly time you have to use that talent to help others. Everyone's purpose on earth is to help others. (Deborah's NDE)

I know that we should try to relieve the suffering of all beings. I know that kindness and a nonjudgmental nature are important. I want to reach out to people. My love for everyone and every animal grows deeper and deeper daily. (Nancy's NDE)

I "see" others differently—have ever since. I realize we are immortal and that we are all fulfilling some role or roles on our paths. (Marlene's NDE)

Nothing on earth belongs to you any longer, everything is temporary. These are not your children—just roles to play—everything is temporary—your success is linked to the way you played your role—it depends on how did you behave. (Carlos' NDE)

All of our relationships are beautiful opportunities to learn to love. We learn to love by showing actions that give peace, joy, warmth, and security to all we encounter. Any actions that create chaos, unhappiness, coldness, and feelings of insecurity are not loving actions that will help us get closer to God. I think that is why there is so much pain in the world. We haven't yet understood that all the pain is a consequence of being disconnected from our true home and our loving creator. The only way to relieve global pain is through exercising love for our family, friends, and the world.

CONCEPTS REGARDING A DIVINE PLAN AND THE LESSONS WE LEARN

One of the more interesting areas to study is the profound life changes that many NDErs go through after they return to earth. Experiencing an NDE is a powerful motivator and an agent for positive change. Do you recall earlier where I talked about the difference between being human and being divine? One of the strongest motivators for change is to have an NDE and experience a life review. Another one is to understand our purpose and place in the universe. And yet another motivator is to understand that the reality of the afterlife is usually very different from what we have been taught on earth. Coming to terms with the core answers to the most basic questions of existence provides powerful motivation for changing human behavior so that earthly beliefs are congruent with knowledge of the afterlife.

DID SCENES FROM THEIR PAST LIFE COME BACK TO THEM?

As an overview, the answers to the life review are perhaps the most profound in determining the nature of the soul. They allude to purpose and give insight into a greater reality of existence. For instance, one unintended but surprising result concerns the logistics of the question. Many people were confused as to whether the question pertained to only a life review of this life, or if it was referring to past lives or a pre-existence. Many mentioned lessons. Inescapably, the life review smacks of immortality.

Sequentially, most life reviews occur after going through the tunnel. However, there were a few who experienced the life review in the tunnel. Only one person experienced the life review at the time of their accident. No life reviews were reported after encountering the light.

The methods of life reviews are as diverse as the people who experience them. The most common expression was that they saw their life flash in front of them and often this occurred instantaneously. Some experienced flashes like Kodak moments. Many experienced a two-dimensional TV, video, movie, slide show, or photographic snapshots of their lives. A couple experienced the book of life. Others experienced their life review in a three-dimensional movie or cinema. There were a few who experienced a life review in a fourth or greater dimensional format.

It is also interesting to note that several people floated through the tunnel and saw pictures of their life on the walls of the tunnel. Analysis shows that there is a statistically significant correlation between people experiencing the tunnel and a life review. Further analysis shows that the life review and the tunnel are not the same thing except in these few instances. Those experiencing a tunnel are more likely to have a deeper NDE, and that includes a life review.

I began to see events appearing along the surface of the tunnel, like a million large-screen TVs or panels lining the walls, but that is a poor description as to what I really experienced. The events seemed to surround me from all sides. (Benny's NDE)

The content of the life review most often included the entire length of the experiencer's life. The life review was commonly played forward, but occasionally would be played backward. It also could be played in terms of only the good moments, only the negative deeds, one major event, or several key happenings. Most were a balance of the good and the bad deeds of the experiencer's life.

Most life reviews show how interconnected we are with everyone and everything. Most experiencers would not only see their experience, but they would feel the ramifications of cause and effect of all their actions. They would experience the emotion of others. NDErs have the rare opportunity to see how their choices on earth affected everyone else around them.

The NDErs most often judge themselves. Much that is hidden from them on earth becomes known. Many lessons are learned through this process. Some had regrets of not doing more good. Others learned that the focus of our life on earth is judged through the eyes of love. The deeds that mattered were those that we did in compassion and love for our fellow beings. Rather than being a judgment based on fear of going to hell, it becomes a judgment of love and hope.

> *The purpose of the review is not for punishment, but for spiritual growth through understanding the ramifications of our actions, thereby gaining increased compassion for others. (Ron's NDE)*

As alluded to earlier, realizations of past lives or a pre-existence came most often during the life review phase of the NDE. There were approximately 9% of NDErs reviewed who experienced events suggestive of reincarnation, pre-existence, or immortality.

> *For instance, we attended a Christian church. This experience "taught me" about reincarnation. I had never heard of the idea or belief in reincarnation, but since I came back I can accept no other belief system. (Sandra's NDE)*

Most of these individuals experienced reincarnation. Many saw lines of people waiting to be reborn. Some knew they had been on earth before, while others wrote about being a product of their choices in this life and prior lives.

> *I was shown a long line of experiences in other realms of realities and in other worlds. It was some time later I realized it was my past "lives" review of all existences of which I had*

been part...past lives review in other realms of existence. (Wayne's NDE)

I was then given the choice to stay or return. I chose to return. But what I can never forget was or is the divine love, the creation, the creator. I somehow knew that we are rein-carnated many times and that the plan is for us all to evolve into that pure love here now. (Erika's NDE)

Some people knew that they had been in heaven before choosing to come to earth. They referred to their experience as being "back home." They did not refer to past lives, but did talk about their choices regarding their life on earth. Many talked about seeing beings who were fa-miliar to them from a life before their earthly life. Inherent in the discussion of reincarnation and pre-existence is the concept of the immortality of the soul as opposed to the physical body we currently live in.

Am I dead? Then gentle laughter, no, Nick, you can't die, you were never born. Is your shell going to die? Not yet. (Nicholas's NDE)

I recognized that I knew him before I came in here, into this body. I felt real happy being with him. The more that I looked at him, the more that I saw how long I knew him. (Tony's NDE)

So, how does it all fit together? What is the pur-pose of life? NDEs show that we are much more than our bodies. From the life review, one of the primary purposes of the soul is to learn lessons and evolve towards becoming an unconditionally loving being. It is <u>very important to remember that everything we do on earth will have a ripple effect.</u> We can feel the effect of every word and action as it touches every person we have ever contacted, directly or indirectly. Because NDErs can see their lives from this perspective, they do change—sometimes radically change—their behaviors, like a modern-day Scrooge after the visit of the Ghost of Christmas to Come. The behaviors they change are those that are not in tune with what they experienced on the other side. They become more loving, kind, compassionate, and giving towards others. Again, these changes give important clues on relationships and soulmates.

WAS THE EXPERIENCE CONSISTENT WITH THEIR BELIEF SYSTEM AT THE TIME OF THE EXPERIENCE?

When asking an open-ended question about whether the experience caused changes in the NDErs' belief system or if there were any behavior changes, the number one change had to do with religion. Many people may have answered this question, but in order for there to be a meaningful discussion, they had to narrate whether a change occurred and, if so, what was it.

The study of NDEs has historically been placed into the paranormal category. Science found it medically inexplicable. Religion wouldn't claim it as a valid experience despite the fact that so many people report the NDE as a religious or spiritual experience. The changes that NDErs go through are directly attributable to such a profound human experience that defies earthly explanation.

Most NDErs unequivocally said that their experience was not consistent with prior beliefs. The explanation could be as simple as reading about NDEs and not experiencing a tunnel, to being an atheist who met God. This is such a broad question that overwhelming consistency in answers to the question makes the answers much more valid than if the answers were all over the board. Here are some comments by NDErs about the difference in what they believed and how those beliefs were changed after they had their NDE:

I know that God isn't some meanie that sits on a throne with a big book and when we die checks off our names and sends us to heaven or hell. (JoAnn's NDE)

Well...I don't see heaven like I used to! No wings! No halos! (Dove's NDE)

I have no doubts about life after death, no doubt that there is anything I can do that will separate me from the love of God. I have huge faith, understand the connectedness of all that is or will ever be. The ripple effect of each act and how everything that happens is interlaced to make a perfect whole. (Sharon's NDE)

The curious thing is that he didn't make me feel guilty. I had attempted suicide and he spoke to me as if I had made an unimportant mistake and he counseled me to do better. (Gloria's NDE)

I no longer fear a judgmental God...one that is looking for reasons to exclude me from Heaven. I now see the beauty in his creations, and know that he wishes for us to be joyful, loving beings while we experience his creations here on earth. (Jim's NDE)

Many NDErs had their existing faith and their religious beliefs strengthened. Many intensified their religious efforts, from going to church to praying more. There were many NDErs who reported that they were more tolerant of all religions because there is no "one" path to God. Some NDErs said that there is no heaven or hell. Others reported that they were more spiritual in their religion. And still others reported that they did not believe in the teachings of world religions because those teachings did not coincide with their NDE. They concluded that since God is love times a million, "love" is the true religion of earth.

We are all headed to the same place, just by different "highways." (Tom's NDE)

I have gotten more involved with my church and celebrate people's death more for being with Jesus and God than feeling sad. (Diane's NDE)

I think [church] should be used to help others feel loved and realize a common and uniting goal. (Maria's NDE)

There were a few people who were told by religious leaders that their experience was of the devil. So many of these experiences talk about the love of God and bring people back into religion, yet others cause NDErs to become less religious and more spiritual. While it would be easy to dismiss some of the hellish NDEs as being of the devil, it doesn't make sense to say that experiences of such love and peace that lead people back to God are of the devil.

We also had several atheists and agnostics who became part of organized religion or more spiritual. While a few of these NDErs are not willing to go so far as to acknowledge God, they do admit there is a higher order or "something greater is out there."

I have to say that I consider myself an atheist. . . I feel that I crossed the frontier between life and death, and there were physically present people who were already dead. (Ricardo FV's NDE)

Other changes in behavior were the lack of fear of death that caused NDErs to live their lives differently. For instance, several were surprised about reincarnation and realized they can make life choices. Several came back with renewed vigor in living their lives. Many changed their focus of life. Some focused on learning, while others focused on behaviors that were more loving and tolerant of others. Others found great joy in helping others.

I learned there is a plan, a reason we are all here. I know there is far more to life than any of us are aware. However, we may not be capable of understanding it while in our current form. I have a much more balanced life. (Sammy's NDE)

Of course, you cannot go through this and not be changed. I have no fear of death, for me or others. In fact, I really have a hard time grieving for those who leave. (Leslie's NDE)

After my experience I started to question a lot about life. I began to follow my inner voice through meditation along with the voices of others...I understand that we are all connected and that there is not one ultimate power but shared universal energy. (Thomas' NDE)

The inconsistency of what NDErs saw and experiences on the other side as opposed to what they knew of earth was the motivation to change. NDErs changed their earthly lives to be more consistent with what they learned from or experienced in their NDE. From the NDE wisdom, it doesn't matter if you give love within organized religion or not. Love permeates through everything we do regardless of whether it is labeled as "religious acts" or "spiritual acts." Again, learning about love is the most important reason for being on earth.

CONCEPTS REGARDING PURPOSE OF EARTHLY EXISTENCE

Most NDErs said that the main reason that we come back to earth is to learn how to love and help one another. Many NDErs came back because they had a purpose or a mission. Some knew what the mission was, while others did not know. Some NDErs were told what their purpose was, but were not allowed or able to remember it upon coming back to their body. A few NDErs had no idea why they were sent back. Another common answer was that our purpose is to learn lessons. A few stated that their purpose was to prepare for their next life. Everything is interconnected, and we are all a part of a greater design.

I learned that the life (here) was merely a method of increasing knowledge/experience for your actual existence. (Brian's NDE)

I was told that I HAD to go back because I had some lessons to learn. I didn't want to go back. (Linda's NDE)

He sent me back, saying it wasn't time for me to be there yet and that I still had lessons to learn on earth. (Pat's NDE)

Various reasons were given for particular lessons. Some felt that the reason to come back to earth was because of duty and work still to do. Others felt that their mission was to increase their spirituality by trusting God and being more tolerant, accepting, patient, forgiving, kind, and appreciative of others.

Some NDErs indicated that they came back to "do good," accept responsibility for their choices, and to live better, fuller lives through concentrating on building positive relationships with children, grandchildren, and other family members. A surprising number of NDErs came back for their children or to have children. Some came back to protect or help family members. There were several NDErs who were to share their NDE with others so as to lessen others' fear of death. Many NDErs stated that their mission was to teach others.

On the flip side of purposes is how the NDEr will learn lessons of love. The largest set of answers had to do with difficult physical handicaps and chronic pain if the NDEr returned to their body. Some were shown that they would experience suffering, pain, cancer, alcoholism, or drug addiction.

When I woke up I was devastated. I had a glimpse of God's paradise and now I was back in my body, sick, hurting, and with a multitude of problems to face. (Nellie's NDE)

Others were shown a hard life or hard work upon return to their earthly body. A hard life meant tough lessons regarding divorce, domestic violence, protecting children from sexual abuse, and problems maintaining a significant relationship or steady job. As one NDEr put it, "Dying was the easy part, living was hard."

Another theme was that once the NDEr experienced heaven, he or she had a hard time staying on earth. These NDErs experienced loneliness, isolation, feelings of inferiority, depression, disappointments, sadness, and unhappiness. These feelings are in such sharp contrast with heaven that the NDErs would longingly wish they were back in heaven. Some NDErs said it was hard to go through the motions of living on earth when they knew it was not real.

I began to cry. It was literally as if I were yanked right out of heaven. I went into a deep depression for a couple days...Worst part is feeling separated from the love. (Shawna's NDE)

The reasons for returning to earth can be summed up as the NDErs chose to learn more about the different aspects of love. Most of the ways to learn more about love are through inter-actions with others. Sometimes NDErs who have the most tremendous handicaps learn the most about love. So the duality of earth does motivate us to transform our consciousness through love, sometimes to the point of going through the fire to purify us for the afterlife.

THE HUMAN CONDITION

The concepts regarding the human condition are those that have to do with the duality and hardships of incarnation on earth. These con-cepts are prayer, judgment, forgiveness, guilt, sin, evil, the devil, fear, war and peace, earthly ill-ness, handicaps, and suicide. NDErs give us hope of a better future. They help us to understand that earthly emphasis on some concepts is misplaced. NDErs give us insight on how to love and trust in a higher power to overcome earthly obstacles.

CONCEPTS REGARDING PRAYER

According to NDErs, prayer has elements of timing and connection to God and involves our earthly will. During the NDE, most experiencers would pray to God, while only a few would pray for Jesus to save them. Most prayers to God consisted of pleas for help, protection from hell, to stay on earth, forgiveness, or acceptance of death. Some NDErs were able to hear the prayers of others or see the prayers as beams of light in heaven.

"Pray," came the voice shouting in my head. I suddenly understood that peaceful voice whispering to me at the beginning of this long ordeal. It had said, "You will die, but do not be afraid! Wait, have faith, fear not, pray." (Linda's NDE)

Then, I started to hear the prayers of all the people that cared about me. My wife, Pauline Morin, my older neighbors, my mother, my in-laws, and my brothers and sisters. I could hear their thoughts and prayers as if they were right there with me. (Anthony's NDE)

Finally, I came to the end of the beam and stood there in the fog and looked up toward Heaven and cried out, "Help me! Please help me! Either bring me back, or for pity's sake let me go, but please don't leave me here." (Sandra's NDE)

There were little beams of light shooting from earth into the heavens, and I asked Him what they were. He told me they were prayers. (Elsa's NDE)

Many people reported that they pray a lot more after their NDE. Most often these prayers were a way to maintain that connection with God that they felt in their NDE. These people reported meditation in conjunction with prayers, with the most often expressed sentiment being gratitude.

Many NDErs were altruistically motivated to pray for others or the world; most often for healings.

CONCEPTS REGARDING EARTHLY FEAR

Fear is one of the major emotions experienced on earth. Fear can be a good thing or it can be bad. Fear triggers the primal instincts of fight or flight. Fear can warn us of danger so we survive as a person or as a species. On the other hand, too much fear can paralyze us, where we just freeze. Fear can keep us from developing to our highest potential of interfacing with the divine. It can also keep us bound to earth and from exercising free will. Without free will we are just a body, not a spirit.

About 13% of the NDErs reported some aspect of the experience that was frightening. Generally, if there was a frightening aspect to the NDE, the NDEr felt fear or terror. This fear may have been momentary until he or she got their bearings and understood they were actually dead, or it may have lingered throughout a hellish experience. The NDEs were analyzed to see what made them feel fear.

The highest reports of fear had to do with the dying process. Either there was a crime, suicide, the NDEr was disoriented, or they were not ready to leave this earthly existence. A few didn't understand that they had died or what was happening.

A couple of NDErs reported that they were afraid they couldn't get back into their bodies.

The next largest group were those who met total darkness. They couldn't see or find their way out. Occasionally this would be a peaceful void, but more often, the NDEr had negative feelings associated with the darkness. There were several who reported a negative, dismal void or a dark, vast nothingness. The negative feelings reported were being terrified, feeling exposed, torment, loneliness, isolation, no sensation, being alone, cold, black, despair, loss, sadness, anxiety, annihilation, depression, no hope, resignation, restlessness, evil, confusion, feeling fragmented, feeling totally separated from creation, and failure.

> What I do recall, and can still recall, was finding myself in the blackest black, cold void, with a crushing feeling of being utterly alone, despair, and loss. There was no sense of anyone else being there, no light, vast nothingness. Terrible. (K's NDE)

> Then I knew I was somewhere else. It was frightening and I didn't understand. I was in a void, no sensation whatsoever, and though it scared me it also felt safe. No cold, no heat, no sound, no beginning. and no end...yet I was looking and saw nothing. (Ally's NDE)

Commonly described places that evoke fear are the edge of a cliff, a deep abyss, a deep hole, caverns, a vortex, a ditch that extends forever, or falling down a well. Other situations causing fear are being in limbo or in hell. Several indicated fear of the biblical judgment. Things and beings associated with darkness and evil also evoked fear.

Beings can cause fear if they are unknown or associated with hell, such as the devil, demons, angel of death, grim reaper, or other biblical figures like an angel with the face of a lion. Creatures that cause fear are snakes, worms, lizards, demons, monsters, and spiders.

Sounds can cause fear, such horrible noises, screams, cries, agonizing pain, moaning, and evil laughing. Smells that cause fear are putrid smells or the smell of rotten flesh. Sensations that cause fear are those of falling, being consumed by fire, being crushed, conscious but not able to move the body, held down, being confined, being pulled, pushed, or suctioned downwards, or creepy things crawling on the NDEr. And, of course, the things of nightmares are flames, blood, bones, and body parts.

Other events that caused fear were one's own funeral, the future of one's children, or the future of the world.

As you can see, there are a lot of ways that people can describe fear or what causes fear. Yet, in the light of love, fear cannot exist. I believe that fear is the number one cause of unhappiness. Many times people don't even realize that fear is at the core of some destructive or other negative emotion. One of the best ways that I've seen to deal with fear is a book called *Feeding Your Demons: Ancient Wisdom for Resolving Inner Conflict* by Tsultrim Allione. The technique is an ancient Buddhist type of meditation. The principal is based upon working with images from the subconscious to change the emotions attached to certain fears. The empowerment and resulting happiness is really worth the read if you want to reduce or overcome fears.

CONCEPTS REGARDING JUDGMENT, SIN, GUILT, AND FORGIVENESS

The terms "judgment," "sin," "guilt," and "forgiveness" imply that we are given a choice to do right or to do wrong. If we fail to make the right choices, it is a sin, and we may feel guilt and ask for forgiveness. Traditionally, "judgment" means a balance sheet where good deeds are weighed against the bad deeds to determine where a person goes in the afterlife. According to the NDErs, the only application of these concepts is a personal one, which helps to foster personal responsibility rather than having society or an outside force dictate and judge your actions. If we lived in a society of pure love, all of these concepts would remain an obscure footnote in a dusty history book.

Most NDErs judged themselves and may or may not have been in the presence of another loving being. The concept of judgment is more like a debriefing after a difficult personal exam on classroom earth. It is important to "do good works" and not to just avoid doing bad things. NDErs judged themselves according to their choices and how those choices affected others. There was definitely a sense of accountability and taking responsibility for their choices. Several times the NDEr was sent back to "set things right."

At the end of this life screen event, I was not left with anyone telling me, "You sinned! You're a sinner! You did this and this and this that was bad and against the Ten Commandments!" Rather I was left to form an opinion of the life. Not so much in terms of "I was a bad person, good person," but rather, "That was a good life," as objectively as though I were commenting on a special meal or the completion of a project that pleased me exceptionally. (Brian's NDE)

I always remember what I felt was an in-depth "conversation" about free will and learning that we all have choices and things that happen, both positive and negative, come out of those choices and they have to be. Some of it I didn't like and while it's a struggle for me to sometimes understand, I realize it happens because of choices. This was in the realm of good and evil. (JoAnn's NDE)

The being was not judging me in any way during the life review, even though I saw a lot of shortcomings in my life. It simply showed my life the way it had been to me and loved me unconditionally, which gave me the strength I needed to see it all the way it was without any blinders, and let me decide for myself what was positive, negative, and what I needed to do about that. (Lisa's NDE)

Man is the only creature that utilizes the cause and effect model in making decisions. By using ego to interfere with the universal cause and effect patterns, it creates a complete imbalance between man and the universe. (Bill's NDE)

The ultimate outcome of judgment was not heaven or hell, but rather how individuals can make choices to better themselves and others. Only 6% of the experiencers had someone else pass judgment, with only three NDErs experiencing the biblical "judgment." I suspect that the most loving way for the divine to interact with these four individuals was to show them familiar concepts. Although "Judgment Day" was mentioned several times, usually it was to say that their experience was the opposite of their pre-existing earthly belief of a religious "Judgment Day." One of the more interesting aftereffects of going through a judgment is that most people report being more tolerant and less judgmental of themselves and others.

The lack of experiencers mentioning forgiveness would imply that forgiveness is more of an earthly concept than one of heavenly origin. Forgiveness implies guilt, wrongdoing, and judgment. However, when NDErs did mention forgiveness, they talked of being forgiving of others, God is forgiving, forgiving themselves, or they were simply "forgiven." Many times forgiveness was mentioned in conjunction with love, compassion, and tolerance. Understanding the plight of others made it easier to forgive. Several NDErs indicated that there was nothing to forgive, rather that they needed to live a good life in order to move closer to God and stop reincarnating on earth.

I am more compassionate, forgiving, and nonjudgmental. (S.K.'s NDE)

Likewise, guilt appears to be an earth-imposed emotion. It didn't come from heaven. A discussion of guilt usually came up in the context of a life review or religion. In the context of a life review, the experiencer would feel guilt or shame at something he or she did or didn't do. This would provide the motivation to do better when he got back to earth. Guilt from religion is imposed on people to control social behavior.

Also surprisingly, there was a lack of discussion about sin. This implies that this is a concept of men and not necessarily one of God, at least in the traditional religious sense that many of us were taught. According to NDErs, sin was more often equated with self-judgment and feeling bad for making wrong choices to act or not act. There were issues of imperfection, earth being the place of sin, consequences for behavior, personally taking responsibility for ourselves, and guilt for wasting time on earth. The more crucial lessons involved total knowledge to better discern the difference between loving and unloving actions on earth. For instance, "original sin" was equated with man becoming aware enough to make choices. The separation of wheat from the chaff was the soul ascending like a rocket and the fuel cell dropping off like the chaff. Only the wheat of the soul would make it into heaven. The soul passed from the sin of earth into a heaven of love and forgiveness.

I felt as though I had come home. From perfection to be born into sin, live in imperfection, never fully understanding the wonder of God, and then finding yourself at his door as he welcomes you in. (Mark's NDE)

From the NDE point of view, judgment, sin, guilt, and the need to be forgiven are earthly concepts. The life review points out that the only things that matter in the transition from earth to the afterlife are the love and loving acts we do on earth. The truth is that our earthly life is about love; it really is that simple.

CONCEPTS REGARDING EVIL, SATAN, AND DEMONS

Only 3% of the NDErs mentioned evil. Considering that the NDE is the most powerful of earthly experiences and evil is only mentioned in such a small percentage of the NDEs, it seems that evil does not exist in heaven, in proximity to pure love, or as a part of God. Most often evil is not explained, but rather a quality attributed to something. The largest group associated with evil was personified as demons. Only a couple of NDErs saw the devil. Several times the devil or evil was contrasted with good and God, such as when the NDEr was being judged.

Evil attributes were described as menacing, scary, dark, or ominous. Sometimes evil meant that the entity had the intent to scare, mock, hurt, destroy, annihilate, suffocate, or cause pain to the experiencer or others. Evil was associated with dragging to the dark, causing to fall, trying to pull the NDEr down, or trying to keep the NDEr from the light. Evil could be a feeling. Evil sounds are those that scare.

Demons generally invoked fear when the NDEr saw them or felt them. They would appear dark, menacing, fearful, ominous, evil, and with no goodness in them. They moved in ways that threatened the NDErs, such as going to harm them, kick, punch, suffocate, inflict pain, torture, rape, or drag into the darkness. Demons taunt, mock, grab, lunge, and cause feelings of hope-lessness, discomfort, or fear. Many times they stay in the shadows, but occasionally will come out flaming and foaming at the mouth. They make hideous noises like screaming, buzzing, or evil laughing. Many times they can appear in forms that humans generally consider as fearful, such as a hairball with teeth, spiders, snakes, or men-acing shadows.

> As the object drew closer, I noticed that it was a fantastic demonic creature sur-rounded by flames with huge eyes and teeth dancing toward me drooling and growling. There was menace in its gaze as it gnashed its teeth and stuck out a long, slobbering, orange tongue. (Sarah's NDE)

> Then I felt like I was pushed back into a wall and my arms pinned back to the wall. I felt totally helpless and then I saw what looked like a hairball with shark teeth come at me. I looked to my right side and saw that the voices were little monsters. (Joe's NDE)

It is harder to understand the nature of the devil because so few people talked about it. Some people described the devil as the op-posite of God or the ultimate demon in human form. Several described the devil in conjunction with God and the final judgment. Sometimes the initial perception of the devil wasn't really the devil.

During this review, the evil being was there. I looked at him. He was handsome not ugly. Black hair, medium build, dressed in a black robe and black cord at the waist, his eyes caught my attention. They were a void! There was no life or goodness in them. (Alexa's NDE)

I looked past them to another light being, so beautiful but darker in contrast, as was the sprawling robe it wore. This being had eyes that pleased but pierced with its gaze, and the light being said, "That is he who has been cast out." (Lou's NDE)

For the first nine months as I dealt with this internally I assumed I was wrestling with the devil; I've since examined it further and know the opposite to be true. (K.C.'s NDE)

Over the years, I have personally struggled with such questions: How do you reconcile such a loving God with such misery on earth? How can evil and God exist together? Many people have said that evil is a part of God. I don't think so. God is the universal creative force of the universe and can take on human form or any other form he/she/it wants. If God is pure love, then neither evil nor any kind of negativity can exist in proximity to God.

If one uses the analogy of earth being a place of dualities and man having free will to choose, evil becomes easier to reconcile with God. We are separated from God, pure love, and this fragmentation in conjunction with free will allows us to spiritually develop. We either make choices that bring us closer to God, or choices that take us away from God. For those people who make more choices to take them away from God, these choices have less energy or light than choices to move toward God.

On a spectrum of choices, those people making negative choices on earth move towards the evil side of the earth duality spectrum. Over time, the evil thought-form continues to capture people and can even become an entity by the power of thought—hence, Satan. Satan can be a conglomeration of people's thoughts or it can be a real entity taking on the thought-form of Satan. We have NDEs where the light being becomes what the NDEr is most comfortable with, so why can't a being of darkness take on the persona of Satan? The bottom line is that God is pure love, while I believe earthly evil is created by man or a consequence of being separated from God.

I don't know what to make of the story of angels being kicked out of heaven. In keeping with the pure love of God, I don't think these angels were "kicked" out for "disobeying" God. Negativity cannot exist in heaven. I think they had to choose the experience of earth.

CONCEPTS REGARDING EARTHLY ILLNESS/ HEALING (EMOTIONAL OR PHYSICAL)

About 16% of the NDErs commented on aspects of healing and illness. The majority of the experiences talked about the illness, surgery, or accident that caused the NDE in the first place. However, along with these maladies were numerous descriptions of miraculous healings that doctors couldn't explain or didn't predict. Many experiencers woke up cured or healed faster than normal. Some had a knowing they would be cured, while others were told that their lessons on earth were to learn how to heal themselves. Several talked about being healed of cancer. Interestingly, some people actually saw spiritual beings or felt spiritual energy healing them during their NDE. Several people contrasted their experience with earth. For instance, a couple of people noted that they didn't need their earthly glasses to see perfectly in the NDE state.

The love these beings of light exuded healed me, swept away all the darkness in me, erased all of the pain and sorrow I'd accumulated during my life on earth. (Lisa's NDE)

I emerged from the hospital the next day, after my parents had been assured that I would be paraplegic at best and that I would have suffered long-term brain damage from the trauma to my head/ neck. I never had even a bruise and have gone on unscathed to graduate from college with no adverse side effects. (Jennifer's NDE)

Oh yeah, I have forgotten to tell you that the Dr. wrote on the front page of my medical record, "Supernatural Intervention." (Roy's NDE)

You must understand that before this experience I had a history of depression and anxiety, and had [anxiety] episodes of being homebound because I was so scared of everything in general. All that stopped with the NDE. (Patricia's NDE)

Another aspect of healing had to do with abilities that NDErs reported after returning to earth. Several reported being able to heal people or going into job fields related to helping others. Healing could occur through prayer, a higher power, hands-on healing, spiritual healing, energy healing, or having increased empathy with and for others. Jobs that help others were typically reported as nursing, massage, hospice work, psychology, and raising children.

When I returned to work, it always seemed that my patients seemed improved while I was there. Does this sound crazy? Honestly, I would begin to "test" it—after I noticed this happening. (Barbara's NDE)

Another interesting aspect is understanding what illness is and how it relates to our existence on earth. Many people reported that the experience of being ill taught them acceptance, learning how to cope, learning empathy for others, and gave them and others hope. The heroic act of an individual choosing to experience illness also opens the door to learning how to heal herself or himself and others. Fear of death seemed to be an impediment to healing; yet lack of fear of death inspired one to heal.

> *I was shown how illnesses start on an energetic level before they become physical. If I chose to go into life, the cancer would be gone from my energy, and my physical body would catch up very quickly. I then understood that when people have medical treatments for illnesses, it rids the illness only from their body but not from their energy so the illness returns. (Anita's NDE)*

> *Knowing that I no longer feared death helped in my long road back to health. (Terence's NDE)*

About 11% of experiencers had handicaps of some kind, either before, during, or after the NDE. Several talked about drug or alcohol addiction. Many of these NDErs were able to break their addiction habit and had completely changed their lives around after the NDE. Several talked about their life disabilities or severe depression that caused natural death or death by suicide.

After the NDE, many of these NDErs reported that they still had their mental or physical illnesses, but many were better able to deal with these handicaps because they realized that there are important lessons to be learned.

It was going to be a very weak, sick female body, but it was what I needed to experience, what I (the spirit) needed in order to grow spiritually. (Sylvia's NDE)

[I] have just recently received a provincial award called "The Courage to Come Back" (award given to people who have come back from addiction or mental illness). (Linda's NDE)

I used to drink. I haven't touched anything since. (Valerie's NDE)

Even our health or illnesses are lessons to learn and exercises in love. When we exercise our choice to love and be closer to God, we are healed. When we don't love ourselves and others, then we have "dis-ease." I know that may sound trite, but it is a powerful concept that NDErs bring back for us. This health may or may not be on a physical level. Many times overcoming illness or pain has led to a more loving and compassionate individual. Life on earth is about love and reconnecting with God.

Prayer is important because it is one of our connections with the divine. We are able to lift our voice to connect with others through prayer. Judgment, guilt, sin, and forgiveness are concepts that we experience on earth and apply only to ourselves in order to make us reconnect better with God in the afterlife. On earth we have fear, illness, evil, and the earthly perception of the devil to contend with. Yet with all of these negative and horrific conditions, the ray of hope is love. None of these conditions can live in the presence of love.

From the NDE studies, God is pure love and light. There may be memories of earth, but all is seen through the lens of love, that is, God's love. The closer we emulate God with pure love in our hearts, the less we are affected by the negative emotions of earth. There are no human attributes that survive the transition into heaven except those associated with love. This includes all the negative emotions like hate, anger, judgment, jealousy, and the like.

This means that what we need to strive for on earth is to emulate love, love ourselves, and love others. This is the goal of a soulmate relationship. We need to strive to reduce or remove negative emotions so that we reconnect with God. How do we do that? The rest of the book will concentrate on relationships based on NDE wisdom, psychology, and personal observation.

PART II: WHAT DOES A HEALTHY RELATIONSHIP LOOK LIKE?

There are many concepts about what soul-mates are and how they are supposed to look, feel, and act in today's society. I have been actively studying relationships for over a decade now. Some of the experience comes from working on divorces and being a guardian ad litem for children. I read a lot about psychology and how best to make a relationship work or to minimize the harm of divorce on children. In order to make better-informed reports to the court, I also needed to know a lot about toxic relationships and domestic violence. Then, there is the NDE work and how the NDErs describe relationships worldwide. And lastly, there is an actual part of the NDERF (www.nderf.org) website devoted just to soulmate relationships where people share their stories with us.

From research and the evidence, there appear to be different types of relationships and reasons for relationships. There are soulmates who travel together through time. Other soulmate relationships are karmic, dharmic, and twin flames. I will explain these concepts below. The popular soulmate who everyone relates to is what we see in the media—the twin flame. This is the public perception that there is a perfect "other" that everyone dreams of meeting, that "love at first sight" moment.

One part of relationships has to do with our nature as human beings. Generally, those people in our lives will mirror a part of us back to us like a mirror square in a disco ball. We can perceive in others that which we know to be true in ourselves. This is one of the bases for the psychology of projection. A great example is when I see a client who comes into the office and she says her husband is cheating on her. Then the attorney who represents the husband tells me that the wife is the one who is doing the cheating, and the husband has been faithful all along. So because of the wife's unfaithfulness, she projects the behavior onto the husband, when it is really she who has the problem.

Another example is one time when I had a trial and represented a hard-working single mother who was having problems making financial ends meet. The judge actually said that she was sick and tired of hearing how my client didn't have any money and then proceeded to bury her in financial obligations to the grandmother. I'll bet that the judge came from a wealthy family and never had financial problems in her life. She simply couldn't perceive poverty in another individual because she never saw it or experienced it herself.

The first type of soulmate is one who is on the same spiritual level and could be part of a soul-cluster group that learns lessons together. This soulmate is a category derived from consciousness studies. Commonly in near-death experiences and after-death communications, the beings encountered or communicated with are most often blood relatives. The nature of the communication and DNA link between the experiencer and blood relatives shows that the relationship is one that transcends time and earth. Many experiencers talk about traveling in a group, then learning lessons on earth together, like a role in many plays. Usually, these soulmates are in a blood family relationship on earth. Many times these earthly roles would be described as a father, mother, daughter, or son; But not always. Sometimes you do see non-blood relatives like a stepparent or a friend. Sometimes the two are romantically inclined, but then the relationship more likely would be a karmic, dharmic, or a twin-flame type of relationship.

A karmic relationship is one where lessons are learned and can span this lifetime or several lifetimes depending on your belief system. The oldest and easiest way to remember a karmic relationship is the saying, "an eye for an eye" or "the Golden Rule," meaning that there is an action and equal reaction in a relationship. So if a person has traditionally been a mean person, then his or her relationships probably don't have a lot of love. These people will either attract someone who helps them to be nicer and therefore spiritually grow with love, or they will not grow and will attract someone who is co-dependent or just as mean as they are. Most soulmate relationships are karmic in nature, where we will continue to attract the same type of person in our lives until we learn a particular lesson. Many times this is a very painful process, and only when people have had enough pain will they make the choice to change.

Romantic relationships and family relationships provide the most potential for change and determine the character of the individuals. For example, the core parent/sibling relationships set the stage for karmic interaction with others. This can be how people resolve conflicts at work, how they act, or how they choose partners for a romantic relationship.

The romantic relationships are usually the most intense because of the mirror principle. Most of the time our coping mechanisms have shut down some or a lot of our ability to love others or ourselves. The slings and arrows that we endure from others as we grow up help us to build a protective cocoon around our emotions so we don't get hurt. The emotional feelings attached to learned protective behaviors are in a holding pattern, rather than flowing as they should. This creates a blockage in the flow of energy. When we are in a loving relationship, the love from inside of us starts to move the emotion again. The habitual behavior patterns reemerge. In order to grow and release the emotional blockage, we have to consciously see what the patterns are and then choose to change those particular behaviors. As each emotional blockage is removed, our cup is able to hold more love. We are able to receive love and give love, until we are reunited again with God.

Another type of soulmate relationship is known as dharmic. These relationships are the people we meet in our lives who help us. Along the lines of the karmic relationship, these are people we have been good to or who we attract into our lives to help us because we have learned a particular karmic lesson and are ready to move on to the next step of our journey on earth.

Twin flames are, in my opinion, perhaps the most intriguing of the soulmate categories. Twin flames are supposedly the same soul, but when they came to earth, they split into a male and female person because of the duality of earth. I didn't know what to make of this and initially thought it must be a romanticization. Then I got a couple of twin-flame stories. Like everything on earth, I've learned never to say "never." So I think twin flames exist, but are not like what the popular media portray.

In order to meet a twin flame, there have to be elements of timing. If one person is married and the other is not, there could be intense feelings of knowing each other, yet no way to be together. I've also heard that twin flames still have fights and arguments. They are learning lessons together. So it isn't that perfect, idealized picture from the Cinderella stories. They still have to live on earth.

LOVE AND RESPECT

Here is a quick review of an insightful study on respect and how it figures in relationships: "Respect in Close Relationships: Prototype Definition, Self-Report Assessment, and Initial Correlates," J. Frei and P. Shaver, *Personal Relationships*, 9 (2002), 121–139. Interestingly, marriage counselors hear about the two main issues in a marriage as being love and respect, but respect and aspects of respect have never been scientifically studied or defined until now. The core relationship values are defined as respect, commitment, intimacy, and forgiveness. The study by Frei and Shaver moves the realm of respect away from the emotional and places it into the realm of an attitude towards "a particular person based on his or her perceived good qualities."

Respect has long been regarded as the opposite of contempt. "Implicit in contempt is a view of one's partner as beneath dignity and essentially beyond the reach of rational discussion" that can be measured by "noticing wrinkles of disgust and upward eye-rolling, two very dismissive gestures. When a person has contempt rather than respect for a partner, there is little the partner can do to get his or her feelings and needs taken seriously."

This study supported findings in Lawrence-Lightfoot's studies, published in her book *Respect: An Exploration* (2000), where she delineated the six qualities that earn others' respect amongst their peers. The qualities are: 1) dialogue ("real communication"); 2) attention ("being fully present"); 3) curiosity (being "genuinely interested in others—their thoughts, feelings, and fears"), 4) healing ("nourishing feelings of worthiness"); 5) empowerment (enabling others to "make their own decisions," nurturing their "self-confidence and self-reliance"); and 6) self-respect (helping others "feel good about themselves").

The qualities identified by Frei and Shaver "included being honest, being truthful, listening to the other, hearing the other's viewpoint, being accepting, and fostering the other's freedom and development." Another finding was that respect is often a mutual exchange whereby if one person respects another, the other person returns that respect. Likewise, if one person disrespects another person, that disrespect is returned in like kind.

I was intrigued by the reasons a person would engage in disrespecting another person. The Frei and Shaver study states that the core reason for disrespect is one of avoidance of intimacy and dependence on partners. A person would be less respectful of a partner for one or both of two reasons: 1) avoidance caused from prior negative models of attachment figures, such as contempt behaviors learned from parents during childhood, and 2) that avoidance as a defensive strategy based upon prior attachment relationships. Failing to fully respect romantic partners may be one way to "avoid becoming emotionally close to and/or dependent on them."

Dr. John Gottlieb is one of the leading relationship experts. He did a study with hundreds of couples which involved watching their interaction over a period of 15 minutes. Then they had followed up on the couples many years later. The study found that there is a rhythm of communication between couples. The ratio of positive to negative interactions should be 5 to 1. Gottlieb's team had accurately predicted 94% of the couples who would get a divorce. The power of positive interactions shows loving, and healthy communications.

On the other hand, there are negative signs that a relationship is over, according to Dr. Gottlieb. These signs are apathy, stonewalling, and living parallel lives. Apathy means that a person just doesn't care enough to argue any more. Stonewalling is a form of throwing roadblocks up to any progress that can be made in a relationship. Leading parallel lives are where the couple lives as roommates, but they don't interact enough to be a romantic couple. This is very common when one or both partners are workaholics, travel a lot, or live apart.

The bottom line is that respect fosters closeness and intimacy with another. Disrespect will cause the other partner to emotionally distance himself or herself and become independent in the relationship. This is truly a shame because the NDE truths show we are here to experience God's love on earth. An impediment to getting close to others is an impediment to soul growth. Further, it deprives the person and those around him or her of ultimate union and co-creation with God.

RECOGNIZING DYSFUNCTIONAL PEOPLE

Dysfunctional people are those who have some sort of handicap to bonding properly with other people. Most of the time 95% of these types of behaviors are learned from the ages of zero to the teenage years, with 85% of the behaviors learned from the ages of zero to five. Most of these people can rehabilitate themselves to have loving and fulfilling relationships with others.

The two principles in relationships are: 1) to follow the energy, and 2) pay attention to what part of you people in your life mirror back to you. All relationships, including those with animals, depend on what type of energy you project. One of the best examples I can think of is from Cesar Millan, the Dog Whisperer. People seem to be pack animals at a core behavioral level. Most people are raised in a family, extended family, or some sort of family substitute such as school or a gang. In a group setting we learn many skills for interacting and survival.

There are the pack leaders, and then there are the followers. I never truly understood this principle until I got a puppy. What started as this little bundle of joy got really big in a short amount of time. My sixty-pound, six-month-old mastiff started to exercise dominance over the other two large dogs. I was beside myself and didn't know how to handle the dog aggression that she was developing. I went back and forth with myself whether I was going to keep her or give her away. Ultimately, by watching *The Dog Whisperer* on a nightly basis, I did not want to pass my problem on to someone else. I took responsibility and kept her. And I'm glad I did.

In the journey, I learned to carry myself like the "pack leader." I thought that as an attorney, I knew how to project my presence to command respect in the courtroom. But was I in for a surprise. I went into a group meeting with that newly learned energy, and everyone was deferring to what I said and looking at me during the whole meeting for leadership. It was a humbling experience to understand it was a type of energy I was still projecting. I learned how to command my own energy to control the mastiff, and it does carry on to groups of people.

Cesar makes the point that if you want to fix your human relationships, then start with the relationship between you and your dog. This is excellent advice, and I now understand what he was talking about. People follow _energy_. He also advocates that in order to be the pack leader, you need to establish rules, boundaries, and limitations toward the other pack members. Again, this is excellent advice, because many people don't impose rules or boundaries on people around them. This opens them up to being controlled and unwittingly dominated, and then putting up with abuse or becoming emotionally hurt.

Remember the mirror principle discussed earlier? Many times, in order to recognize toxic people, we need to look within ourselves. If we are projecting victim energy, then we will attract rescuer energy. If the energy is not balanced and is unhealthy, what one often sees is the energy dynamics of domestic violence in various degrees. Domestic violence is not about the violence; it is about control—dominance energy. As soon as the victim projects a different type of energy, then the relationship changes and even ends. Then another person comes into their life who better mirrors the new energy projected by what used to be the victim.

I wish that schools would teach courses on relationships. It would cut down on divorces and help people realize that relationships are not what popular culture has ingrained into us. It isn't the fairy tale or the dysfunctional, but entertaining shows on TV that turn us into voyeurs of the spicy predicaments the hero and heroine find themselves in. TV as a dominant source of occupying time is geared towards a young audience, and roles played by movie stars become the heroes children emulate. Needless to say, I don't have to worry about job security with almost half the marriages in the United States ending in divorce.

Education is what the public needs to make smarter choices. We spend a lot more time buying clothes, a house, or researching the next computer to buy than we spend researching relationships. Make sure to find out about a person before giving your heart to him or her. Understanding the purpose of relationships and how they work will go a long way towards being happy and learning about love.

Naiveté is a large problem in beginning a relationship. There are a surprisingly high number of people who feel that their soulmate is around the corner and everything will be perfect when they meet. Then when they do meet their perceived soulmate, they superimpose their hopes and dreams of the perfect person over the person they meet. The fantasy is furthered by the rush of "love" chemicals our body produces when we are in love. What a perfect high! The couple may rush into a relationship after being fooled that the relationship is the real deal. This can lead to marriage or further bonding. Then the reality of the relationship starts to dawn on both individuals. The person who they fixed their hopes and dreams onto is not the person they envisioned. Another problem with naiveté is that when one partner perceives the other as an answer to a prayer, many times reason and common sense go out the window.

Toxic relationships are particularly difficult. Since mates don't come with instructions, if we get suckered into a toxic relationship, this can damage us for a long time or even for life. Hence, they are toxic relationships—bad for us. It may take a long time to get away from the poison that they bring into our lives. Some relationships are mildly toxic, while others are major hazmat incidents.

Toxic people are usually very good at disguising themselves. Most of the time you won't be able to spot toxic people immediately unless they are socially inept, so pay attention to actions rather than words. These will give subtle clues. If the actions towards others are gracious and loving, then the potential mate probably is as he or she appears. If the actions toward you are a dream come true, yet the toxic person demeans the waiter for some small slight - pay more attention to the person's actions towards others. Another way to notice people is to watch the syntax in their language. Syntax is the way a person puts a sentence together. It involves choice and order of words. Sometimes, it is off just enough to reveal an ulterior motive.

Most toxic people are masters at spotting innocent or weak people to prey on, and are more likely to be the ones interested in your pocketbook. But unless these types of personalities are understood for what they are, they cannot be avoided.

UNHEALTHY EGOS AND UNDERDEVELOPED OR NON-EXISTENT EMOTIONS

Many people are aware of the experiments with the baby monkeys whose mothers were not available to give them love as babies. Many times the baby monkeys died. But for those who survived, there were severe emotional handicaps. They can't bond or interact with other. Sadly, humans have the same problem. I remember when the school in Moses Lake, Washington, was devastated by a teenager who shot and killed many of his classmates. I remember Columbine. It was very illuminating to have Christine Gregoire, attorney general of Washington at the time, talk to members of the state Bar about the findings of the committee she headed regarding violence in schools. The number one problem was that the shooters were children who were not properly socialized and given love from their parents between the ages of zero to three.

Unfortunately for singles looking for mates, these babies grow up. They either totally lack the ability to bond or they have minimal bonding skills. For those who had minimal love growing up, they can sort of bond, but can never quite develop the emotions enough to experience love. Emotionally handicapped people will have a tendency to create havoc in their relationships or will be emotionally apathetic. They may have an inability to maintain a long-term relationship. The inability to love in a healthy relationship will make that person keep the significant other at a distance. And the significant other has enough emotional issues that he or she chooses to stay in this type of relationship. Many times, the relationship is abusive or is more like parallel lives without any emotional interaction between the couple. There may also be a pattern of behavior arising in the family of origin that kept the person from emotionally developing properly, such as one or both parents in the domestic violence spiral or addicted to alcohol and/or drugs.

With underdeveloped or nonexistent emotions comes an unhealthy ego. They go hand in hand. "Unhealthy egos" refers to people with self-esteem issues, meaning overblown self-esteem or little to no self-esteem. Unhealthy egos, underneath it all, do not love themselves or respect themselves enough to mirror a healthy, loving, soulmate relationship. I know, it sounds a little paradoxical that people with self-absorbed, inflated egos do not love themselves. Consider that if they did love themselves, they would have the confidence to mirror love in their outside world. Many are scared to death to let their emotions show because that means a loss of control. They don't respect themselves enough to trust that they can control the situation outside of their head.

CONTROL

Power and energy abuse stem from the need to control self and others. Controlling people are those who feel the need to mold their environment into a preconceived idea in their head. This need manifests in manipulation of the people and events to conform them to the controlling person's preconceived ideas. Many times controlling people have had disappointing or highly competitive childhoods. A good description of abuse of power is as follows:

The abuse is obvious. A superior [in their mind] crushes subordinates with power. It's also often a way for a petty tyrant to increase self-esteem. To compensate for a fragile self-image, they need to dominate; their ability to do so is made greater when the subordinate is afraid of losing [something important to them] and has no choice but to submit...In theory, abuse of power is not specifically directed at an individual; it's simply a matter of destroying someone weaker.

Adapted from *Stalking the Soul, Emotional Abuse and the Erosion of Identity* by Marie-France Hirigoyen, pp 67–68.

The more pathological the need for control, the more destructive to others it becomes. In the extreme situations, control may involve destroying the significant other to make him or her conform to the "ideal" other in the controlling person's head.

Earlier, I mentioned that the cornerstones to a soulmate relationship are love, respect, and trust. One reason that a controlling person in a relationship cannot have a soulmate relationship is because he or she does not have the ability to love, trust, and/or respect a significant other. In their mind, the only person they truly trust is themselves because that is the coping behavior they learned to get what they wanted as a child. That is what they know. Most do not even know they are controlling and will adamantly deny it. Rather than empowering others, controlling behavior is geared to disempowering others to more easily control them.

Pathologically controlling people have such a strong concept of their "ideal" world in their head that anything that deviates from that "ideal" does not pass the threshold barrier of the brain into conscious thought. Controlling people define their ideal person or situation in their head and expect the other person to conform. The significant other is, in reality, an extension of the controlling person's ego. When the significant other does not act or say what the "ideal" significant other would, it is either not heard or there is a fight. The fight becomes a power struggle where the controlling person must win in order to make the other person reconform to the "ideal" in his or her head.

Controlling people are unable to have soulmate relationships because they do not love and respect the significant others for who they really are. Many times controlling people are incapable of real communication because they can't or won't hear the other person. Furthermore, any attention they may show is focused on themselves. They are curious about others only to the extent they can learn how to control them. As I mentioned before, controlling people cannot empower significant others because then the controlling person couldn't control the significant other. Controlling people are incapable of helping others to emotionally heal, since they have little or no emotional empathy.

Sometimes a controlling person is benign. They simply don't realize they are acting in a controlling manner. Love and willingness to change is as simple as making one aware of the behavior. In others, the need to control can be so strong that they may never shake themselves loose enough to truly love another person.

MANIPULATION

Manipulation is a way to control others to conform to the manipulator's will. Manipulation comes in many forms, but the bottom line is that the person is like a sheep in wolf's clothing. He or she will play mind games to exercise power and control over another person.

I think that everyone to some extent has the ability to manipulate others. The difference is when this exertion of power to get what we want becomes extreme or is used by someone with little or no empathy. Empathy is the ability to feel what others feel. At the extreme end of the spectrum, a psychopath or sociopath is incapable of empathy, so he or she is very adept at manipulating others. These people don't feel remorse or pain inflicted upon others, so they are capable of inflicting unspeakable horrors on others.

Manipulative people are always trying to control a person or situation. They can use any number of ways to get another person to do what they want. Many times they can make the other person feel guilty, threaten an undesirable result if the other person refuses to cooperate, or they can use any other unpleasant consequence like extortion or blackmail. These scenarios are extreme manipulation, but they do exist.

The best way to avoid manipulative people is to pay attention to what they say. Don't hear what you want to hear, but really hear what they are saying. The manipulative behavior probably won't surface right away, but you will see signs of it. For instance, they want ice cream but don't want to leave the house. They ask you to go get them ice cream. You don't want to go either. Then they start to pout and make you feel guilty. So you go into the freezing blizzard to get the ice cream.

CODEPENDENCY

Codependency is marked by a lack of being able to stand on one's own. Generally what you see with codependency are people who are afraid to be alone and have low self-esteem. These people feel like they need to have a signifi-cant other and will generally choose someone below their expectations because the codependent person doesn't feel worthy of love. These people cling to others like their life depends on it, the fear is so pronounced. It is also not surpris-ing that codependent people will attract either abusers or other codependent people.

One variation of this relationship dynamic can be the rescuer/victim mind-set. The rescu-er is always ready to step in and help a person he or she feels needs rescuing. Generally, the rescuer has good motives, but may have low self-esteem in relationships. The victim is one who always seems to be abused or in a bad situation a lot, the "oh, poor me" syndrome. Many times the rescuer is looking for someone to be grateful to him or her and the victim is looking for someone to whom to be grateful. Unfortunately, this dynamic can be the start of a relationship with a power imbalance because they both can be forms of codependency. The relationship will go sour when the victim no longer worships the rescuer or the victim becomes stronger than the rescuer.

In order to overcome the cycle of codependency, codependent people need to become aware of the fear and to overcome their fears of inadequacy and loneliness. By cultivating love and compassion towards others, and having the courage to set rules, limitations and boundaries, these people will be able to overcome codependency issues and to attract the soulmate relationship they have always wanted.

DESTRUCTIVE NARCISSISTIC PERSONALITY DISORDER (DNPD)

The story of the ancient Greek myth of Narcissus tells of a young man who so admired his own reflection in the water that he fell in love with his image, but when he tried to kiss it, he fell into the water and drowned. This was the result of being so in love with himself that he ignored the love of several women and angered a goddess. This story was used to warn young men from being so engrossed in themselves that they are cruel to their female lovers. Ironically, when a person has DNPD, he considers himself too perfect so he doesn't hear or need to heed the warning of the goddess—to be nice to his mate.

Unfortunately, this type of disorder is the one that frequently rises to positions of power, such as doctors, lawyers, CEOs, and politicians. They are incredibly hard working and understand the art of manipulation for power, fame, and money. They usually don't have a lot of emotions, so this makes many decisions towards others seem heartless. Since those with DNPD have less-developed emotions, they will often observe how others react to what they say or do. They quickly learn to manipulate others strictly on an intellectual level based on this feedback loop.

People with DNPD are masters of control. They are also most likely to be highly intelligent. Argument is futile because they can manipulate anything that is said. The end result of argument is to win, and they will say anything to win. Many arguments are won because they keep raising the bar or framing the situation in a way that the target is damned if they do answer and damned if they don't answer.

The reason that this diagnosis is "destructive" is that in order to maintain control, a DNPD person must demean the other person. That means that he or she needs to destroy another person's will because control is so important to them. Many partners are lured into the trap of a person with DNPD because the security, money, or fame is so tempting. But because of the lack of empathy in a person with DNPD, this is essentially a Faustian deal with the devil. Even though a partner may get something out of the relationship, it is at a heavy cost to their soul.

The only way to survive in a relationship with a DNPD personality is to not react to anything he or she may say and keep emotions level. That also means one must have firm boundaries and not allow the DNPD person to breach the perimeter of those boundaries. Rarely will a DNPD person go to counseling or a psychologist, because the DNPD person believes that any problems are caused by the significant other.

It is extremely rare for a DNPD person to change or even realize that they need to change in order to be in a happy relationship. Therefore, it is probably best to avoid these types of people. You can apply the ten-minute rule to recognize them. If you spend ten minutes with them and you don't get to talk or the conversation is all about them—walk away. Even the most skilled DNPD personalities can't stop talking about their interests or themselves for a long period of time.

BORDERLINE PERSONALITY DISORDER (BPD)

Run the other way! These people create chaos and disorder in the lives of whomever they touch. Generally, they are very social and charming. They are the people who are probably the most entertaining and outgoing at a party. They attract people to them like moths to a flame. And that's exactly what happens to those human moths—they go up in flames because those with BPD are amazingly deceptive and destructive underneath their entertaining and social façade.

People with BPD are great storytellers and may have little or no regard for the truth of what they say. They remind me of a black widow or a scorpion, because many people can't tell when they are in the enchanted web or about to be stung. BDP people can be amazing con artists or would be great double agents, so hold onto your pocketbook tightly around these people.

People with BPD most often have extremely bad, abusive childhoods with little or no love. They may have addictive personalities that have end goals of being adrenaline junkies. They could enjoy gambling, alcohol, or drugs to find that adrenaline high and enjoy mind manipulation with their significant others, like "cat and mouse" games. For instance, I have known several people like this who will worm their way into the boss's or significant other's good graces and find out all the dirt on them. Then when the relationship goes sour, the BPD person will attempt to destroy the other person by publically exposing them.

These people you most likely can't detect by intuition. The best way to detect them is by their actions. So make sure if you have a charmer on the hook to ask a lot of questions and pay attention to things like stability in past relationships or jobs. They usually can't hold jobs or are players who can't stay in a committed relationship for more than a year or two at a time. Everything they touch has drama and chaos attached to it. I best remember BPD by analogizing them to the "scorched earth" policies of warfare where everything they touch is destroyed.

DOMESTIC VIOLENCE (DV)

This is an entire subject that has many different facets. But rather than being a crime of violence, it is all about control. Many times these people either have grown up in a home with DV or cannot verbally express themselves when they are angry. The result is that they resort to physical violence in order to be heard or maintain control. Mental and emotional cruelty can also be part of the domestic violence cycle.

I know that many people consider that DV is one-sided. Actually it has many different facets and is mainly one-sided in only the most extreme cases of DV. From what I have seen, it takes two to have domestic violence. And for most cases it isn't one-sided. I have represented both victims and perpetrators in divorces. Many times what I saw was that the victim was a mental aggressor and the perpetrator was the physical aggressor. Both were aggressors, just in different ways. The physical aggressor was the one who got thrown in jail, yet the laws didn't do anything to the mental aggressor. The end result was who was going to control whom and by what means.

Stalking and possessive behavior are different. Stalking is an obsessive behavior where the focus is on the other person. This can be very dangerous because compulsive stalking and possessive behavior can lead to death. The highest incidence of death in a domestic relationship is when the breakup of the relationship occurs.

In order for these people to come out of the domestic violence cycle, they need to learn to love themselves and others more. They also need to be empowered so that their low self-esteem rises. The courts will typically order anger management behavioral modification. If there are also issues of alcohol or drug abuse in conjunction with DV, then they need to overcome their addictions, too.

Another consideration is that one person might be fine, but in the wrong relationship—such as one with a borderline personality disorder person. Getting away from a BPD and allowing more love into their lives may be all that is needed to overcome a DV situation.

ADDICTIVE BEHAVIORS

These groups of individuals have destructive, compulsively addictive behaviors such as drugs, alcohol, food, gambling, or even sex. Some people believe that these people are victims of their genetics and those addictive behaviors are diseases. Regardless of whether addictive behavior is inherited or environmental, these behaviors drastically interfere with a person's ability to love another person. Many times these addictive behaviors will lead to forming codependency relationships.

In order for these people with severe addictions to be able to find a soulmate relationship, they first need to control their demons—usually the best method is through twelve-step programs and peer group support. They need to love themselves and work on self-esteem. Then they will be able to attract the ideal soulmate into their lives.

BIPOLAR DISORDER AND DEPRESSION

Bipolar disorder and depression are mental diseases that can be controlled with medication. Many times people don't realize that they are bipolar when they are manic for a while and then depressed for a while. These people are on a constant roller coaster. Depressed people can be debilitated by depression and may lack drive or energy to perform basic functions such as getting out of bed and brushing their teeth.

I include these in the group of toxic relationships because these people cannot be in a soulmate relationship unless their brain chemistry is under control. With proper medication, these individuals are capable of giving and receiving love. But without proper medication, they can be very much like people with addictive behaviors or borderline personality disorders. They can either be a listless person, or a listless person with destructive tendencies.

BUT DON'T THEY NEED LOVE, TOO?

The host of emotional disorders manifested in toxic behaviors includes but is not limited to personalities of psychopaths, sociopaths, destructive narcissistic personality disorder, borderline personality disorder, addictive behaviors, domestic violence, and victim mentalities. These emotional disorders can easily be recognized by noticing the commonalities of control, underdeveloped or nonexistent emotions, and an unhealthy ego driven by the need to feel important. The specific disorders are the reflections of different ways of coping with the lack of love or the inability to experience true love. These disorders foster various forms and degrees of contempt towards partners to avoid emotional closeness.

Toxic behaviors give dysfunctional people the power they crave, at the expense of the other person. They also help release the frustration and stored negativity from the toxic person and triangulate them to another. "Triangulation" is a fancy word for releasing negative emotions onto another person who is not involved in the relationship. That is why they are called toxic behaviors—the negativity and destructive emotions created from a life of chaos or creating bad will come spewing forth towards a vulnerable person who absorbs it. The energy is so bad that it actually poisons a vulnerable person.

The short answer is that those who exhibit toxic behaviors need love more than most people, but they are rarely able to accept love. They can only recognize in others that which they see in themselves. Sadly, they don't see love like a normal person would. Their stunted emotions prevent them from recognizing love normally. The only way for toxic people to change is to have a major life event where they hit rock bottom. This forces them to look at their situation and starts the wheels of change. They have that five percent option (that part of the brain that is not programmed out of habit), to change their destructive behaviors. Then they are able to spiritually grow if they choose to do so.

But this is a book about how to find your soulmate now. You can only find your soulmate if you can recognize another person who is capable of growth, love, and compassion. That means that you have taken responsibility for yourself and are looking for someone who is already at a loving soul level, rather than someone who would need to change.

PART III: SOULMATES

One of the biggest questions is echoed in the Sammy Hagar/Van Halen song, "How do I know when it's love?" The million-dollar answer is as expansive as it is elusive. For instance, love means many things to different people. Just ask someone what he or she thinks about intimacy. You will get answers from emotions, to sitting on a beach sipping cocktails, to total indignation about "how dare you ask such a personal question!"

I think that when you know "it's love," then you have found your soulmate—but there can be many stops, starts, detours, and bumps along that road. There are no easy answers because there are several types of soulmates. So if you really think a person is "the one," it could be a karmic soulmate and the lessons may not be quite what you think love should be. Additionally, there are chemicals that create loving feelings, and there are other emotions that may seem like love. Remember the mirror principle? We see that in others that we can see within ourselves. There are also ingrained patterns of behavior from when we are under five years old that govern how we interact other people.

Now we get to put it all together and start to look at the "soul" in soulmate. The purest form of love that we can find on earth is what the NDErs tell us from their encounters with the divine. That is the love that we all search for. We all search for that collective consciousness or remembrance from whence we came. We come from a place where love is magnified a million fold from what we experience on earth.

This is the part of the book that gives you a warm fuzzy—and gives us motivation to become more than just ourselves. Earlier I talked about NDE wisdom. It is no coincidence that those who have experienced God and love firsthand without being fettered by earthly bonds—are the teachers. We are fragmented from God when we are born to earth, and trying to regain that lost love is a core motivator and part of the collective human consciousness. We are all trying to be reunited and reconnected with the love from whence we came. Consequently, the lessons we learn from making correct choices to allow love in our life help reconnect us with God. We reawaken our soul and the remembrance of coming from a place of pure love.

Soulmates are one aspect of the NDE lessons because the very qualities that we see in the NDE are the ones that we feel when we meet our soulmate or soulmates. The NDErs describe incomprehensible love that we can only glimpse here on earth. Soulmates describe that same intense love and connection. This love is unlike anything else that we know on earth, yet brings us the closest to reconnecting with God.

As I mentioned earlier in the book, soulmates come in several ways and for several reasons. There can be many soulmates of different relationships to us and they can be either gender. There are karmic soulmates we learn lessons from and with. There are soulmates who are helpmates. And then there are the twin flames, which are a part of our soul. The relationship can also take many forms. Soulmates can be part of our soul or part of a soul cluster group we travel through time with. These people can take on the role of our significant others, casual acquaintances, family relations, or co-workers and neighbors.

With this as a backdrop, I was primarily looking at the soulmate stories submitted to and posted on NDERF (www.nderf.org). The most information received on soulmates was in the romantic and significant-other category, so that is the focus of this part of the book. However, you will notice many crossover concepts that are common to all types of soulmates and in all types of soulmate relationships.

The strongest qualities to come out of the study were eternal love, instant connection, a true friend or companion, and the sense they had been together before, such as a prior life or the preexistence. The soulmates talk about a deep understanding, trust, having the same beliefs, and an immediate strong connection. Upon meeting, the connection was known by both partners; there were no stories where the soulmate connection was only known or felt by one person. This connection is on a soul level and may be accompanied by a spiritual awakening or opening to a higher consciousness. Not uncommonly, the first sentence or meeting revolves around spiritual matters and both partners feel the resonance. Many comment on the difference or uniqueness that the relationship has when compared to prior relationships. Others talk about how the relationship completes them or makes them feel whole. The other qualities are more traditional, such as joy, happiness, high commitment to each other, infinite tenderness, hope, compassion, honesty, faithfulness, respect, treasuring every moment together, and unconditional love.

Soulmates can meet just about anywhere since there is usually a predetermination about meeting. By that, I mean there is usually a signal, sign, or unusual coincidence that brings about soul recognition in soulmates. This meeting seems to evoke a strong knowing or soul memory. The most common place that soulmates in the study met was on the Internet. Some met at college or high school. Others met at social gatherings like a public lounge, bar, dance, concert, swimming pool, or a party. And still others met through their jobs or through attending conferences.

There are also some amazing coincidences involving predetermination. For instance we have a woman from Fiji and a man from Jamaica who met in the United States. What are the chances they would meet out of millions of people on the planet?

Another soulmate story was submitted by James. He had a NDE-like experience where he was told to "wait for little Pebbels" and that she was coming to him soon. Furthermore, he was told more information about her such that he knew that they had the same birthday and were soulmates before walking the earth. Three days later, they met. "Pebbles" was her nickname that her mother always called her. Even more synchronous, her mother said that God told her to nickname her little girl Pebbles so that the right person would know that she was the person he was looking for. It turned out that that Pebbles was born on the same birth date and time that James was born. This is one of the closest soul mate stories that might suggest a twin flame where one soul splits into two halves.

There were a couple of surprises to come out of the study. At least they surprised me! There was a higher than normal percentage of people who knew from a young age (pre-teenage) about their soulmate, either through dreams or even an imaginary friend. There were also several people who dreamed or wrote about their soulmate prior to meeting him or her. Many times this was a mutual dream or knowing. A high number of individuals met their soulmate either as children or teenagers or in the golden years. There weren't very many who met in the middle years. These are curious trends, but then again, they are derived from small numbers. These trends would need further study before anything conclusive could be said.

In these dreams, he always wore a striped shirt and said he would wear a striped shirt when we met...When we met, he was wearing a striped shirt. After we met the dreams stopped. (Marie)

The NDErs talk about recognition of being home, connection, and knowledge. This all occurs on a soul level, too. So it isn't surprising when people talk about meeting their soulmates. Here's how some experiencers described their soul recognition:

I don't know whether it was what people call "love at first sight"; all I know is we belong to each other – we always have and we always will. (Penny)

When we met, it was gradual and instant... gradually knowing this person again and instantly recognizing that this was the person I was looking for. (Peggy & Jeff)

It was like drinking pure water when one is dying of thirst. My fainting soul has been nourished by both these individuals over [the] years. (Samantha)

When I look back on the first moment that I laid eyes on her, even then I knew the connection we had. (Rich)

I saw two specks of light in this deep space, understanding those lights to be two souls searching for each other through space and time. (Bua)

It's hard to explain but I felt like we had always known each other. I knew he was IT. (Pam)

We felt the universe suddenly open up to us as if someone pulled a string and the curtain went up. It is a spiritual awakening for both of us. (Yvonne)

You've heard some of the common phrases about meeting, like "electricity flowed through us" or "sparks were flying." There is a physical basis for this, and it resides in the union of like souls. Harmonic resonance occurs when two identical energies combine and amplify the energy of both sources.

For instance, I have a soul sister. When I was younger, the only thing that would save me was prednisone. For her, prednisone was the cause of her NDE. We discovered at a conference that when we put our hands together, the energy between us really magnified and a lot of heat was generated. In many ways, it was like a yin/yang complementary energy balance, but amplified.

123

This type of physical energy is what can happen when soulmates come together.

We have entire book industries dedicated to romantic fiction. Yet feel the real soul resonate when reading about soulmate meetings:

It was if we were the only two people there. As he looked at me his eyes took a soft warm shape. He was reading right into my heart. He reached his hand out over mine completely covering it. Gently he lifted my hand to his lips and softly laid a kiss there. Lost in this moment I was hanging on every word. "It's a pleasure, my lady." Chills ran over me. It took me a second to comprehend I was holding my breath. (Lisa)

We looked at each other; our eyes locked. (I recognized the eyes from dreams as a child). I swear I saw electricity in the air around her. She was lit up like a Christmas tree. The flow of energy from and to each other was incredible. It scared the hell out of me. (RER)

I walked over to watch them and saw this nice-looking young man standing before the board getting ready to throw the darts. All of a sudden as I looked at him, there was a great voice inside of me that said, "Oh, there you are! I've been looking everywhere for you." (Iris)

Something in his eyes literally "flashed" at me for a split second, and it was a split second of pure recognition. I saw timelessness in his eyes, I saw him as an old man, just for a nanosecond, and I knew he was "the one." It's like his eyes had a life of their own for that instant. (Kammy)

When I met him, I was completely spellbound. I said mentally to him, with a great cry from my inner being, "Once, a long time ago, we were the same person. Then something terrible happened and we were torn apart and we have been trying to get back together ever since!" (Contessina)

This is no joke: we floated in the middle of the dance floor. I mean, I couldn't feel my legs! The lights became a soft blur and everything began to slowly spin; just like in the movies when the camera revolves around the couple. All I could see was her smiling up at me. Everyone in the room vanished. It couldn't have been more perfect. Time stopped for a while. I knew then that I had fallen in love...The first thirty-seven years of my life were in preparation for our union. If I had met Ellen any sooner, I probably would have lost her to all of the mistakes I seem destined to create. (John)

I was there for about thirty minutes and in walks the man from my dream. I was *stunned. My heart raced and I told my friend that the man from the dream I had told her about three months earlier just walked in the door. I finally went and introduced my-self to him...I've now been married to him for eighteen wonderful years. (Rita)*

Anna met her soulmate at work. She said hello to some co-workers and spotted him out of the corner of her eye. Her world stopped. She was totally absorbed in rec-ognition and awe. *Anna shares, "Our first kiss (which was inevitable) felt as though I was kissing myself. I couldn't believe it. When we look at each other there is a li-quidity in our eyes, I seem to enter him, and come back out. Like a flow of our en-ergy." (Anna)*

We can acknowledge that there are many types of love on earth. There is romantic love, compassion, unconditional love, a love that a parent has for a child, just to name a few. When discussing love from the soul, it is a bit different. Here are some descriptions:

Not the same kind of love that one would feel in a romance. It doesn't feel like a human emotion, a longing or need. It's not what I feel; it is a part of me—in my soul. (Donald)

When I first saw her I didn't feel like I was just looking at her physical appearance but rather into the depths of her soul.

Somehow I could see through her and in essence feel her...I feel not only that we are soulmates but ultimately one soul. I love her more than any one man could love another woman. She is my everything; she consumes me and completes me. I am grateful for every moment spent with her, and I look forward to our life together with assurance that we will be together forever and an understanding of what it truly means to be a soulmate in love. (Rich)

You recognize the essence in each other. (Pam)

Living with her is like living on velvet: soft, easy, peaceful. I would describe our relationship as a yin-yang relationship; Complementary. (Robin)

I knew that having met her, even for the briefest time, that all who followed would be measured against what I knew in my heart: a love so true, so pure, and so eternal that I could never love another in that way, an everlasting love deep within, a love that wasn't in my heart but in my soul. (Donald)

Many experiencers describe instant recognition on a soul level and an instant connection with that person. This connection manifests itself in many forms, but it is not uncommon to see descriptions of a psychic bond, telepathy, healing, empathy, and harmonic resonance. Below are a few descriptions about the soulmate connection:

> I'm a writer, and my soulmate said things with the exact same phrases that I would have used; it felt as though I might've written them myself...As much as soulmates complete us, they also challenge us, they keep us on course, they thrust us, headfirst, into achieving what we were put here to do. (Koren)

> One of the craziest things about discovering your twin flame soulmate is how much alike he or she is to you. Not just in liking the same things, but rather in the way you think. The amount of times that we say things at the exact same time are countless. Our minds seem to be in complete tune with each other to the point of predicting what each other is going to say in a given situation or circumstance. (Rich & Martina)

> I cannot describe in words the feelings of immense happiness and euphoria that result when we are together. I have been told that when we are together, it's like nothing else or no one else exists. We share dreams, share words, share thoughts, and along with finishing each other's sentences we learned to write the same, too. (Jenny)

Meeting a soulmate is a feeling of being totally comfortable with who you are in their presence. We have an extraordinary level of communication, but we can also just "be" together without even having to talk. (Pam)

Several people describe telepathy such that they can tell if something has happened to their significant other, they complete each other's sentences, and they can tell what the other is thinking. The nature of the relationship is synchronous, where the sum of the two soulmates is greater than either one of them apart. The relationship is nurturing and allows for healing and growth as a couple.

One theme among soulmates, is needing to learn lessons on earth for soul growth. Many people reported coming out of bad relationships prior to finding the soulmate relationship. Several talked about working on oneself to become emotional healthy after failed relationships. Part of this working on oneself is to make conscious choices to allow love and loving people into one's life. Many experiencers distinguished between these learning relationships as being karmic in nature and different than the soulmate relationship they were currently in. Although some people need to emotionally heal before a soulmate comes into their lives, this is certainly not true for everyone. Many people just happen to meet their soulmate, no matter what stage of life they are in.

Although the relationship or trying to be a couple may not be effortless, the love between you is. Words do not need to be used, and in [your soulmate's] presence you are completely accepted for who you are. Time, distance, and personal struggles do not change it. It has always been. This is what a twin flame love feels like. (Brynda)

I realized I had wasted time in suffering, and what I should have been doing was using my freedom to choose true love, and not pain, in all that came into my life. . . I saw my loved ones were only reflections in the great theater of life and each one voluntarily agreed to play a part in order to learn more and better how to love. (Hafur)

I have been shown what a real connection is supposed to feel like when you meet a soulmate. Meeting others is like looking at cardboard figures now; I couldn't accept a relationship with anyone like that. (RER)

Increased love and connectedness is a result of the journey of healing our past [childhoods] together. (Barry)

I know we are together by preplan. He has grown a great deal and so have I because of our conflicting relationship. Somewhere between us is the right balance. (Julie)

Another theme that comes out about meeting a soulmate has to do with timing. Many people reported that they were married at the time of meeting their soulmate, so they could not be together or they had to wait before being together. Some recognized that even though the person was their soulmate, they could not be together in this incarnation because they had different lessons to learn. Some had emotional barriers, while others had geographical barriers. Several reported that their soulmate was not on earth. Others reported that their soulmate had been on earth, but had since passed over to the other side. While this situation is less than ideal, in the grand scheme of things, the soulmate bond is eternal—so taking a short time apart from your soulmate for learning lessons is not as bad as it appears on earth. Here's one description where love transcends into eternity:

> I asked her, "Will I see you again?" And she said, "Make no mistake, you will see me again. There will come a time in your life, I can't tell you when. But you will open your eyes and I will be there waiting for you, saying, 'Let's go, it's your time.'" Brian

It is interesting to see that soulmate relationships are different than what we typically have been taught about earthly relationships. These are the relationships of the soul and, consequently, the ones that last because of the eternal love between the couple. There was not a lot of emphasis on physical lust, but certainly they refer to intense passion when together and definite "sparks." Soulmates are unique. Many times there are unusual meetings, events that have been predetermined or soul recognition through dreams. They have an intense connection, psychic bond, and immediate recognition of each other.

HOW DO YOU GET A SOULMATE RELATIONSHIP?

The next question you're probably asking is, now that you have read what a soulmate union can be, how do you get one?

If you're single, then finding your soulmate is going to be a fun adventure. The secret is in making positive choices to bring your loved one to you. From the above research, it is hard to tell if you can manifest your soulmate or if it is a predestined meeting. I suspect both are true. On some level it is predestined because it is an agreement at the soul level prior to coming to earth.

I also think there could be an element of meeting on the spiritual planes prior to a physical meeting. This you could do by dream work to try to contact your soulmate on the inner planes. Or you can try manifestation techniques such as writing down your ideal person after meditating for a while. There is also something to the idea of the law of attraction. When you meditate or visualize, not only are you putting your energy out into the universe, but you are changing yourself to realize and recognize your soulmate. Moreover you can send a beacon of energy and create a loving vortex around you that helps your soulmate to find you. Consequently, soul work helps your soul to simultaneously be able to recognize the person as well as to put that energy that attracts your soulmate to you.

If you're in a committed relationship, then the best advice is to know yourself. I never advocate breaking up a marriage if there is any way to avoid it. Knowing yourself has two components. It means to understand yourself, your patterns, and what changes need to be made in order to accept a truly loving relationship in your life. The other part is to be able to honestly evaluate the relationship you're in. Is there potential for mutual positive change? Are both parties willing to work on the relationship? Is it a one-sided relationship? Is there a power imbalance? If people have spent the time to learn about themselves and their own behavior patterns, then they can best understand what they see in others.

Many times there are karmic reasons for relationships. If there are lessons to be learned and a relationship is prematurely broken up, then the next person will help you learn the lessons you didn't learn in prior relationships. All of these observations learned from soulmate accounts help us learn more about our connection to God and how we learn different aspects of love—how to reconnect with God.

Look at basic issues such as compatibility. Compatible means that the interaction with the other person shows compassion, trust, and respect. If there are issues that trespass on these compatibility elements, then have a talk with the other person. Issues can be on both sides. See if there is a middle ground of compromise, or if the other person is loving enough to work through the issues with you.

One issue that might come up is one that is similar when we studying NDE. There is a definition of the experiences that we want to study. The definition helps to determine if the experience becomes part of the research. When we post the experience as a "probable" or "possible" NDE, then people seem to get their feelings hurt because it isn't a NDE. I guess the gold standard of experiences is the NDE and people feel devalued if it isn't part of the research. Let me stress that each experience that a person has is a valid and meaningful experience. Classification is only for research purposes and does not devalue the experience in any way.

Similarly, there will be a lot of talk about the gold standard of soulmates – the twin-flame. If a person has a different type of soulmate or can't tell what kind of soulmate they have in their significant relationship, it doesn't make the soulmate experience any less of a soulmate experience. It simply means that there are different issues to be addressed in each type of relationship regardless of classification.

Two people can transform a relationship into a soulmate relationship. As long as both people are committed to making a relationship more loving, they can both change their energy on earth. By changing their energy together, they can become soulmates and experience that yin/yang balance.

The next chapter talks about the four steps to actualization in the soulmate process. Actualization means that the soulmate union can reach its maximum potential on earth. Sometimes it is necessary to prepare for a soulmate union. As you may have noticed in the research above, there were many who were coming out of bad relationships before they actually met their soulmate. So, there is a way to bring your soulmate to you. What is also interesting is that the soulmate union is a small part of a larger union—that with God. So I have expanded the concept of the soulmate union to include more than just two people.

FOUR STEPS TO ACTUALIZATION

Understanding relationships and their energy dynamics is only one step in finding your soulmate. The hardest part is to actualize this knowledge so that you can have the love and relationship you deserve. I'm going to outline the four steps of actualization to finding your soulmate. These steps are to be honest with yourself and others and to practice love and compassion in a committed relationship and in the world. Sounds easy? It will take a lot of commitment and willingness to make mistakes and to be open enough to change your behavior. It isn't easy at all. In fact, it is one of the hardest challenges most people have ever faced.

BE HONEST WITH YOURSELF

Being honest with yourself means that you are committed to finding the truth about yourself and are willing to change into a more loving being. This means adopting the state of mind to exercise choice in situations that will bring the most love and the least anger or chaos. Remember that every person is a divine spark of a greater light and is deserving of love and compassion. I say this because many people have low self-esteem even though we are all equals in the eyes of the divine.

In many ways, the success of this part of the transformative process depends on using the superconsciousness to be aware of yourself in the third person. This process involves using that five percent part of your brain that is not part of your habitual behavior. People need to be able to notice when they are acting out of habit and work on changing unwanted behavior.

Unwanted behaviors are any actions or behaviors that are not loving. Earlier we talked about loving behaviors and qualities associated with love. Remember that loving behaviors are those that bring intense love, peace, warmth, joy, happiness, ecstasy, compassion, acceptance, calm, completion or fullness, comfort, beauty, purity, security, a lack of fear, forgiveness, safety, non-earthly, goodness, and truth. So whenever a person understands he or she is exercising unwanted behaviors—being mean, hateful, bringing about chaotic, ugly, impure, short-term pleasure at the expense of another person, needing to win at all costs, causing discomfort, acting unsafely, or engaging in bad behavior, violence, and lies—then these behaviors need to be consciously changed.

Noticing unwanted behaviors is a painful process and takes a lot of courage. Don't be afraid to ask for help in the transformation process, but make sure that you don't put your trust in someone who isn't trustworthy. You can use several methods depending on your personality and what you need help with the most. Many people can do this by themselves. Others can't and may need a psychologist, counselor, hypnosis, or a support group.

The goal of working on unwanted behaviors is to release the emotional blockages that have been holding a person back from experiencing pure love. Blockages distort our ability to perceive truth and experience love. They are the reason that we make bad choices and develop bad, unloving behaviors. Most of these blockages come from emotional pain that we didn't process when we were ages zero to five. These behaviors are coping mechanisms from many negative experiences, such as being rejected, demoralized, or abandoned early in life.

When the blockages are released, then we are able to perceive the truth about love. It is rare that there is someone who has an easy time of dealing with releasing blockages, although to be fair, some blockages are easier to release than other traumas.

Emotions are what make us human. Anger, fear, and pain keep us from experiencing love. These emotions separate us from our creator and distort the truth about love. Our intellect, and being able to maximize love out of the chaos of earthly emotions, is what makes us divine.

Emotions are interesting because they don't operate on logic. We have brains that are wonderful at rationalizing why we stay in this relationship or that unhappy job, such as: we may not be able to live on our own, we're afraid of the global economic downturn, we lack the confidence to strike out on our own, or we want to stay because of a duty or obligation. But emotionally, we may be a wreck because of the relationship or job.

Rationalization rarely works on a subconscious level because of the conflicting emotional feelings. These inner conflicts may physically show through dysfunctional behavior, compulsive disorders, little ticks, or other neuroses. The only way to heal is to ferret out the source of the conflict between emotion and intellect. As one of my psychiatrist friends reminded me, he was adamant about needing blockages because they give us safety and protection. So be careful when working on emotions. On the other hand, the harder this is to do, the more gratifying the release of the emotional blockage.

Emotions are much like water in a bucket. They are intense and splash from one side of the pail, and then over to the opposite side of the pail, then to the other side, then to the other side. Eventually, the emotions will be calm as a new emotional equilibrium is reached. In the process, there will be periods where you feel good and then periods where you feel horrible. But each round of splashing from one side of the bucket to the other has less energy with it. Eventually, the emotions will be balanced and calm. Just remember that this is the way emotions are. This knowledge will help you to ride out the bad parts of rehabilitation and be able to make the most of the peaceful moments until you are able to regain balance. There always is another day, and the bad will pass.

One way to know if you are truly progressing towards your goal of being a loving person is to use people around you as measures of your success. The mirror principle works. Take an inventory of the top ten people in your life. Notice whether they bring love and peace or anger and chaos into your life. As you continue your journey of self-discovery and learn to release emotional pain and accept love into your life, you will also realize that people will react differently to you and mirror the love you project back to you. The top ten in your life will either change to be more loving towards you and others, or they will leave your life. Ultimately, you will be surrounded by loving, giving, and compassionate people. But again, this takes conscious choice and willpower on your part.

When looking for a soulmate, spend some time getting to know yourself and what makes you happy. The things that are important to you should be what are also important to your mate. For instance, if a person is an athletic person and being fit is important, then he or she should look for that quality in a partner. I would suggest sitting down and writing what is important to you at home, in a social setting, at work, and so on. This will give a template for what qualities are important to have in a soulmate. It also is an exercise in visualization to help bring your soulmate into your life.

One of the largest love myths is thinking that we have the power to change others. A person may be inspired by our confidence and our ability to love, but the only thing that changes another person *is that person.*

When you run into barriers and life gets stressful, remove yourself from the stress. One of the most effective ways to do this is to concentrate on "love." In the face of love, all frustration vanishes. Do you know the song, "So Small"? I first heard it on *American Idol* when Matt Girard sang it. When I am feeling stressed, I start singing the lyrics, "Love makes everything else seem so small / You might realize that mountain you've been climbing is just a grain of sand," and I calm right down. That mountain really does become a grain of sand when you let love into your heart. You realize love is all that is important, not that stressor at work or at home. When you love yourself, the arrows of life bounce off. They can't touch you.

When people are able to be honest with themselves and work on their own issues, then they are witnessing an amazing transformation in their lives and the lives of everyone they touch. And just as when a rock is thrown in water, the ripple of reactions spreads out and creates more love. Real love attracts real love and a real soulmate.

BE HONEST WITH OTHERS

There are many places to meet others. One can meet others at work, in church, at the grocery store, the Laundromat, at the gym, various clubs and on the Internet. The best place to meet other people is a place where they interact enough to know the person and in a place where it is easy to assess loving and compassionate qualities.

Be aware that dating in today's society isn't a Cinderella story or the 1950s. There are more people, and because of the overcrowding, violence in the mass media, and the rise of one-parent families, this is a dangerous world and you need to be cautious. The best way to talk to someone you don't know well is to never give out any personal information until you are sure you can trust them. Personal information includes but is not limited to your last name, where you live, your phone number, where you work, or any identifying information that your date might be able to use to find you. Trust your instincts. If you feel uncomfortable around someone, pay attention to that feeling. Don't discard the feeling because the person on the other side of the table looks like a mythical Greek god or goddess. Looks can be deceiving. Finding a soulmate depends on knowing the person from the inside, finding out about his or her character and ability to love.

Also meet in a public place to minimize any risk to yourself. Meet at a restaurant, a coffee shop, or other place that has a lot of people around. The first meeting is to explore whether as a couple you two have enough in common to continue to round two—another date. This is where knowing about the toxic relationships really comes in handy. Most of the toxic types are fairly easy to spot with a few good questions. On the other hand, you need to remain careful, because there are some people who are too good to be true. Many times these people are the masters of manipulation and telling you what you want to hear. They will give subtle clues, though. Remember that not everyone is as brave as you or looking for a soulmate. People lie. They may not be as honest with themselves as you have been. You need to keep your eyes wide open and see people for who they are, not for what you would like them to be.

I know in some places and in some cultures that it is considered rude to ask personal questions. On the other hand, you need to be able to assess someone for compatibility. Then again, the new Internet culture has broken down a lot of the normal barriers in favor of speed dating. So, ultimately, don't be afraid to ask about someone's family of origin, such as their parents, brothers, and sisters. This will give you clues to how a person deals with family, if he or she can be in a committed relationship, and what types of issues might come up in a relationship. Don't be so quick to dismiss the stories about the ex-wives or ex-girlfriends. Many times reasons for breaking up will highlight issues in a prospective soulmate. But if the setting or culture doesn't allow for such questions, then just have more public dates and keep private information from being known until you are sure that the other person can be trusted.

Some general things to look for in other people are their ability to love, their ability to be flexible, and their ability for compassion. You are looking for a soulmate but nobody is perfect—otherwise we wouldn't be on earth. That's why the ability

143

to change and grow is so important. If the person isn't flexible, then it probably isn't a soulmate relationship. You want to be able to love, to be loved in return, and to know that you can grow more in love with this person as time goes on. People can only commit to the relationship if they are truly willing to work on issues together.

There are a couple of questions that will give you a lot of insight into someone. The first one is, "What does intimacy mean to you?" The answer will show you about emotional depth or lack thereof. The other question is about prior relationships and why they broke up. Many people don't want to talk about it. That means they probably haven't processed the relationship enough to move on. Or they could be in various stages of grief, such as denial, anger, depression, bargaining, or acceptance. Acceptance is good because then they are ready for a relationship. Look for patterns. And as a family law attorney, I know we need to listen because there are always two sides to a story. Chances are good that the reason for the breakup has a mirror image in the person you're talking to. For instance, if the reason for the breakup is money, then look to see why there was not enough money, and consider issues of stinginess or issues of control. Remember there are always reasons for actions on both sides, and reasons for reactions.

When the relationship has progressed for a time, compare how this person fits into the ideal soulmate list of qualities that we talked about earlier. If the person matches fairly well with your soulmate list, then go ahead and continue the relationship. Don't compromise important, realistic values or settle for less than you deserve. Remember to review the list as you grow. Many things that were important in the beginning of being honest with yourself will change as you become more loving and accepting of others. Continue to reevaluate yourself and the potential soulmate every one to three months. It is much easier to break up within the first three months than to let a relationship drag on for years.

The bottom line is that you will find your soulmate if you remain honest with yourself and honest with other people. Meet people in places where loving and compassionate people can shine, because you'll see these people in an environment where they can love and give of themselves. Unfortunately, the world is not a perfect place. So you have to exercise caution and discernment when you look for your soulmate. Spend time with people and get to know them. Don't be afraid to ask questions so you can see about compatibility and ability to grow in a committed, loving relationship.

PRACTICE LOVE AND COMPASSION IN A COMMITTED RELATIONSHIP

The hardest part of being in a relationship is being honest with yourself and others. We have

145

to take baby steps because change doesn't happen overnight, and there are many stumbling blocks along the way. It takes a lot of courage and persistence to successfully be a loving and giving person.

In today's world it isn't easy to be in a loving, long-term relationship that is balanced spiritually, mentally, emotionally, and physically. Most people have one or two sides of the four-sided pyramid, but cannot sustain a fully loving soulmate relationship. Relationships that are not balanced on all four levels generally are lacking love in one or more areas and these areas will be a constant source of conflict.

Consider that working with a soulmate can also be difficult at first because the closeness to each other causes core emotional issues mirroring back at each other. Working through these issues on both sides can produce miraculous healing and greater love and respect. If a couple isn't mature enough and compassionate enough, they won't grow to experience that universal love. They will stay in a holding pattern and not really go any further. This can lead to a degeneration of the relationship where one person grows and the other does not. This is a common cause for divorce. But if a couple does work through the issues together, it is an amazing transformation.

It can be very difficult to allow oneself to be vulnerable and lay bare personal feelings and hopes to another person. This takes a lot of love and trust of oneself and of one's partner. Each person needs to be open and willing to help the other through issues and to work towards soul callings and life goals. Each person needs to be secure enough in himself or herself to accept constructive criticism in areas that need to be changed. Helpful suggestions can be given out of love.

I had a reader on the NDERF website write to me some time ago. He read some of my articles about soulmates and love. He wrote back amazed that before, he used to look at grilling hamburgers as a chore. But after reading the articles, now he sees cooking hamburgers as a celebration of life where he can give a loving part of himself to his family by cooking these tasty foods. He changed his perspective from one of expectation and chores to one of love and giving.

Everything done out of love remains. So in a relationship we have the opportunity to show our love. Yes, it may be difficult to pick up after oneself or put down the toilet seat. But we do these things out of love and respect for one another. She shouldn't have to fall into the toilet in a groggy, nightly sojourn to relieve her bladder. He shouldn't be forced to pick up her things because he wants a home that is uncluttered. If we look at our reasons for doing things, these issues quickly are transformed by love. When people love other people, they want to make them happy and to give of themselves. I remember a saying that if you love something, you spend a lot of time with it. So, by loving others, you honor them. You spend time with them. Actions that are loving and done with a loving heart have a ripple effect, and they help us connect to our loving, divine source.

The relationship between ourselves and another person is very special. It gives us the opportunity to witness a miracle within ourselves as we are able to remove our blockages and experience more love. A soulmate relationship allows people to work through their issues together. It is like a yin and yang symbol where both partners make a complete whole. This synchronicity sets the stage for transforming the world.

PRACTICE LOVE AND COMPASSION IN THE WORLD

In many ways a soulmate relationship is a preparation to experience love and to give love to others. The next step is to bring unconditional love and compassion into the world. The soulmate relationship is the basis for being able to do this. Imagine if we were able to relieve misery and dispel hate, anger, and prejudice. Love means everyone gets fed, everyone gets love, and there is no greed or raping of the earth for personal gain. Love starts with individuals and goes from there.

Love cuts across all cultures and all socioeconomic groups. I remember when Mother Teresa died. A young Muslim was asked by the media why he was standing in line to pay his respects. He simply said, "Mother Teresa's goodness transcends religion."

I routinely deal with translators from all over the world. The message of love, hope, and peace is so strong in the NDE stories that my goal was to get translations of all the NDE accounts, because the more that love and peace are spread around the world, the more global impact there will be. Additionally, when people realize that we all have the same experiences all over the world, it will also help bring people together. And it has. We have over 100,000 unique visitors per month from all over the world. The NDERF website did grow tremendously with the help from countless volunteers who shared in the vision of peace. The message of love is a powerful one.

We desperately needed peace, love, and compassion in the Middle East, especially with the bombing of the Twin Towers and the war in Iraq. I was trying to get the Arabic portion of the website going. I didn't know much about the Arabic world, and I only knew about Muslims what I saw on TV. That wasn't a lot, and it wasn't good information. It portrayed people from the Middle East as fanatics and Muslims as terrorists.

Then along came Shaza, who had offered to help translate the website into Arabic. She is Muslim and from Sudan. I remember thinking after a few e-mail exchanges that this was never going to work. We didn't have enough in common to communicate with each other. Imagine how I felt when I found out her culture thought dogs were unclean and her surprise when she learned I allowed my mastiff on the bed with me. But the one thing that bridged the gap was love.

Through persistence and determination to make things work, we made it through. When we focused on our commonalities and our families, we found a way to communicate for the greater good. I also learned a lot of patience, tolerance, and respect towards Shaza. It also opened my eyes to the pain and struggling that her culture goes through at the hands of her government and the ripple effect of U.S. dominance in the world.

One suggestion is for everyone to take the challenge of finding his or her soulmate and transforming into a loving, compassionate couple. The energy of two people together is greater than the sum of their parts. If enough people can transform themselves, they can transform others and the world. Love isn't just a word in the dictionary, a Bible, or other holy book. Love transcends from being an emotion to a state of consciousness that connects us to the divine. Loving and compassionate actions, when practiced with intent and in large groups, do have a lot of effect on others.

The more love there is in the world, the more people transform. We need to reorganize our lives so that we don't depend on a monetary system, and we need to prioritize what is important to us. Through the lens of love, all things on the earth and all people are important. Everyone deserves to be fed and to be happy.

If we value life, then it shouldn't just be at birth. We need to value life as people grow up, have families, and get too old to take care of themselves. We need to value the life of animals, trees, and Mother Earth. If we practice love, then all of these values will come to the forefront and enrich our lives, families, and everything or person we come in contact with.

CONCLUSION

We are conscious, sentient beings created with pure love. We come to earth because of the challenges that earth provides. We learn lessons and travel with a group of souls throughout eternity. The way to maximize our time on earth is to overcome these obstacles with love. It isn't easy for most of us. For one thing, few people are born with money or opportunities that will ensure that they have the basic needs of life, so many people cannot concentrate on being altruistic if they need to find food and shelter to survive.

We constantly struggle with dualities and choice; yet paradoxically, these are the circumstances of earth that allow us to grow to our greatest potential so we can return to the loving divine. By looking at the wisdom of the afterlife through the eyes of NDErs, we can understand what our true nature is. We are loving beings, created with love, and then separated from that divine love in order to grow. Our relationships with others show us who we are. We do have the ability to change if we exercise the five percent of our brain that controls creative thought rather than habitual behavior. We can create new, loving behaviors.

Relationships depend on a person's knowledge of what a healthy relationship is as opposed to a dysfunctional relationship. Relationships are about energy, that which we project and that which is projected upon us. There are toxic personalities out there that are incapable of fully loving another person. If we are mirroring energy that puts us in a bad relationship, then when we recognize a dysfunctional pattern and change our behavior, the relationship changes. The ultimate goal of relationships is to learn about love and to give love to others.

With that as a backdrop, get creative with romance. Many people report that there is that something special about their soulmates. It is like there was a predetermined sign prior to birth that both of you would recognize. It could be that the moon was special and the glint in her eyes that triggered the recognition. It could be as simple as her colored hair bow, or a certain look as he exits the soccer field. Many people report that they are drawn to the other person like a magnet, or that <u>when they talk, there is a familiar knowing; like they have known each other all their lives. There is a sense of destiny.</u>

One very large thing that comes up is timing. There may be that special feeling between you both, but one is married. The married scenario comes up a lot in e-mails from readers. I never encourage spouses to break up to follow their "soulmate." The universe doesn't work like that. If the timing is right, then there are signs. Pay attention to the real signs. Most times the signs are fairly obvious, like finding pennies or hearing a certain song over and over when it is no longer popular. The universe has a way of making coincidences, so it is up to us to pay more attention to "soul" signs.

Don't forget to look at the willingness to work on a relationship, because there are lessons to learn in each relationship. Many people may be in a soulmate relationship and not realize it because they don't understand how to be in a relationship.

There are <u>four ways to actualize love in a</u> soulmate <u>relation</u>ship: 1) <u>Be honest with yourself;</u> 2) <u>Be honest with others;</u> 3) <u>Practice love in a committed relationship with your soulmate; and</u> 4) <u>Ultimately share that love and compassion with others.</u> Each step in the process is a way to learn about love by recognizing it and then by giving it to others. Go out and join a group or an organization where you can give of yourself. Volunteer with love, and it magnifies.

We, as humans, have choices that we need to exercise. With a world depression, millions of people out of work and starving, we need to get back to our spiritual nature. There are so many people who are in so much pain, who are in poverty and trapped in a fragmented world. Poverty isn't just monetary. We have poverty in spiritual, mental, emotional, and physical areas. We need to understand that relationships are the most important thing. We need to get back to our families, friends, and our communities. The survival of our species depends on the soulmate relationships we form on earth. And we have a choice.

With enough people, we can change the world one person at a time. Love is a bond of connection, empathy, and communication between oneself and others. It is that oneness that holds the very fabric of the universe together. Especially wondrous is the union of souls when we find our soulmate!

ABOUT THE AUTHOR

For my day job, I am Assistant District Attorney for the State of New Mexico working on a pilot project with State, the County, the City, and the Navajo Nation.

I am an active co-investigator, and writer with the consciousness websites and related projects. I have been involved and actively studying consciousness for over 10 years. Additionally, I am webmaster of three top ranked websites that all show different aspects of consciousness: NDERF (www.nderf.org), ADCRF (www.adcrf.org), /and OBERF (www.oberf.org). I gave the websites a face-lift in March 2002 and have been the current webmaster ever since that time. My dedication to the website and input on directions for NDERF have been important for the growth and research prominence of the websites today. ADCRF has been consistently second on the search engines. OBERF was resurrected and now is doing really well since people all over the world want to talk about and hear about other consciousness events. The NDERF international project is very exciting because it has opened global vistas. Consciousness can now truly be studied on a world-wide basis.

I consider the global message of peace, love, tolerance and brotherhood to be the corner-stone of the message of the NDE and to that end diligently works toward unifying others through-out the world. One of the projects to come from this book will deal with groups, relationships, and "doing good works."

The newest member of the pack is Zara, a Neapolitan Mastiff 2 years old. She's taught me a lot about patience, assertiveness, and being a pack leader. I really love dogs, so this is another of my passions.

In my spare(?) time, I enjoy making necklaces from genuine stone beads. It is very calming for me to use my creative right brain after a hard day at work. I guess I need a lot of calming, because I have made a lot of necklaces . . . So my hobby has now become an online business. www.jewelrybyjody.com.

CREDITS:

Love's Divine Grasp Statue permission courtesy of Design Toscano, www.designtoscano.com

Author and Angel photograph by: Jaycelyn Etsitty

DISCLAIMER:

    I am not a medical doctor or a psychologist. Portions of the book pertaining to any diagnosis are provided for illustrative purposes, not as professional advice. If you encounter any of these conditions, please see your medical doctor or psychologist.

Copyright

Made in the USA
Lexington, KY
02 July 2014